Curious Chronicles from Sri Lanka

By

Table of Contents

Preface 3
Chapter 1 – En Route.. 5
Chapter 2 – Touch Down 9
Chapter 3 – Colombo (Part 1).............................. 14
Chapter 4 – Around Kandy 25
Chapter 5 – Kandy 33
Chapter 6 – The Cultural Triangle (Part 1)............ 40
Chapter 7 – The Cultural Triangle (Part 2)............ 48
Chapter 8 – Induruwa... 53
Chapter 9 – First Day in Galle 61
Chapter 10 – Galle (Part 1) 69
Chapter 11 – Galle (Part 2) 76
Chapter 12 – Galle Day Off.................................. 85
Chapter 13 – Unawatuna 95
Chapter 14 – Mirissa and Blue Whales................ 100
Chapter 15 – Colombo (Part 2)........................... 111
Chapter 16 – The Trains 121
Chapter 17 – Ella 125
Chapter 18 – Train in the Hill Country................ 135
Chapter 19 – Adam's Peak 143
Chapter 20 – Colombo (Part 3)........................... 150
Bibliography 159

Preface

Dear Good Reader,

May I convey my hearty congratulations to you for acquiring this book? Such is my relationship with marketing it is an unlikely occurrence for many people to have learned of its existence so I am happy to disclose that you have already defeated the odds.

You have placed in this book an enormous quantity of trust, probably based on only a fragment of evidence, that the hours you will spend with it will be worthwhile. Your judgement is impeccable and for that I give you my compliments and my thanks.

This book is not a guide to Sri Lanka. Within these e-pages you will not likely find succinct and informative assessments of restaurants, guesthouses and popular tourist sights. There is simply much more interesting and thought-provoking stuff to discover. Instead you will meet a host of eccentric, bewildering and wonderful characters and an account of how people brought up with different customs, laws, behaviours, ideas and surroundings to me live their daily lives.

The aim of this book is exploration... to explore an area of the world that has very different attributes of interest to offer the curious than what England offers, and carries the hope of finding people with different practices, principles, preferences and drinking habits and to understand why they do what they do. This is also an exploration of ideas... ideas that can emerge from existing in strange, new environments that become relevant at the time for one inconsequential reason or another. And who knows, perhaps we might find the inspiration and opportunity to learn something new and fascinating.

'Exploration' is a tool of learning that has no idea what it's doing. It goes about its business inquisitively and inefficiently poking around trying to find something of intellectual worth. It does so with no control or guarantees whether its results will be glorious, tame or non-existent. And yet, the most significant strides in human knowledge have resulted from the thrilling experience of exploration. This book, my friends, by way of exploration forms a small part of that long and tumultuous voyage toward that which we all yearn for… to a greater understanding of our world.

Chapter 1 – En Route

So, I thought as I stood lost in the vast, open expanse of the airport, *I need gate 125. Where am I… hmmm… ah, gate 212. GATE 212!!!*

I knew Dubai Airport would be huge but 212 gates… *Good Lord! That's 87 gates away, each 100 metres apart. Hmmm… that's… 8.7km!? In 15 minutes!? Good Lord! That's some… 35 km an hour I have to travel to catch this plane. Good Lord, that can't be right!* "Quite so, young traveller", the Good Lord didn't offer. Of course it wasn't right, it was absurd, but how could I know?

I had left England 9 hours to my stern with its familiar rules, systems and mannerisms but in these unknown waters my imagination had run wild. No airport in its right mind would make passengers walk 8.7km to gate 125. Shouldn't I have known that?

But out here I don't know what the rules are. Only a fool would presume that everything was the same here as it is back there. And if it was what would be the point in coming? Some things would be the same and some not but I didn't know which. And when those things not the same reveal themselves to not be the same I knew I wouldn't know anything about them. And I didn't know how to know what to do about not knowing what I didn't know from what I did know. *What!?* The simplest way out of this preposterous riddle was to assume I knew nothing.

It was back to square one and square one is a dark and lonely place. It summons feelings of apprehension, anxiety and a slight sense of dread. I felt like a little lost child… and it was fantastic!

One of the wonderful things about being a little child is that you have no idea what really goes on in the world. What truly exists and what doesn't? Ghosts? Tooth Fairies? Fair-minded Bankers? You just could not know for sure what is possible and what is impossible and so, by definition, anything is possible. Any number of wondrous and magnificent dreams could be round the next corner, or conversely, a horrific and terrible nightmare. All terrifying monsters are possible until you eventually learn which ones are real and that most of them are on Big Brother. Either way, the dreaded square one holds a dark and expectant excitement.

Our approach to Dubai airport had already thrown me off kilter, "…and we should arrive in about 30 minutes or so though we're likely to experience some delay before landing. This is the busiest time in Dubai Airport", our friendly and courteous Captain addressed the passengers. "It's 31 degrees in Dubai and the local time is nearly midnight." *Midnight? The Busiest Time? What the hell's going on!?*

He wasn't wrong. The terminal bustled with travellers rushing to their gates, weeping at the prospect of running 8.7km or browsing the many shops (including one ambitious outlet hoping to sell one kilo bars of 24 Karat, Suisse gold to passers-by for £46,000 – "one minute, dear. I'll just nip into that gold shop. Did you bring the deeds to the house?")

The only thing I knew was that I didn't know anything... but then I started to learn.

1. Dubai Airport is enormous.
2. If I spend $1,288.67 on jewellery the gold shop will give me a free scarf, and
3. Gate 125 was just around the corner.

We left Dubai airport passing Dubai's new spectacularly tall Burj Khalifa building; its breath-taking night-time view was gratefully enhanced when our considerate pilot flew us perilously close by to catch a glimpse of ladies getting changed through the windows. With that unexpected treat behind us we zoomed our way towards Sri Lanka and blue whales.

When I was about seven, before my head became filled with guitars and football, I lay on my bedroom floor flicking through an animal encyclopaedia and discovered that the largest animal in the world is the blue whale. In fact, it is the largest animal to have ever lived on Earth. Like all small children that same fact was repeated to me during school, on Blue Peter and within London's Natural History Museum and I vowed to take more notice of it the day I see one.

At the age of seven an hour was plenty of time to do anything, a year was incomprehensible and a lifetime was about the same as an eternity. I casually assumed that during the eons of my lifetime I would chance upon a blue whale at some point and, showing astounding patience for a seven year old, contained my excitement until then.

In the years that followed I concluded, amongst other revelations, that guitars and football were splendid, that a lifetime is not the same as an eternity and that I was unlikely to happenchance upon a blue whale in my resident city of Sheffield in the north of England. It had become abundantly clear that if I wanted to see a blue whale I'd have to bloody-well go and find one.

Even with this recently-acquired vitality blue whales are not easily found. We know virtually nothing about them; where they go, how they behave, what their social habits are and even how many there are. I had often hoped to see an informative documentary with stunning video and absorbing insight but I never did and, if you think about it, it's hardly surprising. Blue whales can be tricky to find when your search starts as narrow as the oceans of the world and even trickier to follow when they dive to great depths at high speed. It appears we have had an easier time putting a bloke on the moon than we have of observing blue whales for any meaningful length of time. They are the mysterious giants of our planet. The biggest animals on Earth and we know hardly anything about them.

It was, therefore, a moment of deep joy when one night, at the age of 32, I watched 'Ocean Giants' on BBC1; a program that presented what we now know about whales with the venerable Stephen Fry narrating the way. The last section of the program took us to a population of blue whales that, Stephen Fry explained, stay in the same area all year round - most peculiar behaviour for a whale. His narration went on... "So what holds them to this patch of blue sea off Sri Lanka? By measuring how temperature and salinity change with depth, scientist Asha de Vos believes she has the answer." A young, confident Sri Lankan woman then explained her theory about areas of upwelling bringing up cold nutrient-rich water toward the surface that attract the whales' favourite food, or something to that effect.

With the news of this population of blue whales and the memory of my nonchalant assertion to one day see a blue whale I knew I had to go. Their location... 10km off the southern coast of Sri Lanka and a village called Mirissa. *And I might chance my arm at finding this young Sri Lankan scientist too.*

I chose to begin this expedition in mid-March 2012 for two reasons. Firstly, from early March 2012 I would be jobless following redundancy, and secondly, Lady Luck in all her radiant beauty had ordained the England Cricket team to ply their gentlemanly trade in Sri Lanka in late March and early April. *Blue whales AND Test Cricket!!* And there was one more addition to make.

I have been to Asia once before. In 2007, I negotiated a month off work and went looking for things I'd not before witnessed in Thailand

and found plenty (one of the last and very memorable events was to see a talented and unattractive woman shoot a dart out of her most private of female valuables with such vigour that it stuck in the ceiling!).

Thailand's other attractions was its jungle, beaches, a welcome disinterest in health and safety and the chance to meet preposterous people of a wondrous variety. It is a country so different to my own that surprises, peculiarities, unusual people and curious situations jumped out from every corner.

A month in Asia was enough to experience almost none of it. Folk told me of their surprising travels around Thailand's neighbouring countries, Laos, Cambodia and Vietnam that sounded more entertaining still. I made another nonchalant assertion to one day go back to South East Asia, if ever I got the chance, to explore its abundance of absurdity more thoroughly.

With a pocket full of redundancy cash and burdened by no responsibilities like a house, job, wife or girlfriend, I extended this jolly to make good that assertion too.

Those sketchy ideas constituted the bulk of my preparation. I included in my backpack a Lonely Planet book for Sri Lanka and another that covered Laos, Cambodia, Vietnam and Northern Thailand. And for entertainment I took a book by the physicist Stephen Hawking, a pen-knife and a harmonica in C with the express intention of learning how to bend a note - a skill with a long-standing tradition of evading me.

Chapter 2 – Touch Down

When I asked the lady at the Bandaranaike International Airport information desk for a pen she delved into her handbag for one of her own. If it wasn't for that local touch I could have been forgiven for thinking I was still at Heathrow. In the airport's clean and air-conditioned interior I read in my Lonely Planet Book that Colombo is 22 miles away and that there were regular buses from a bus station nearby. At 9am I left behind the comfort and protection of the International Terminal and ventured into the real Sri Lanka.

"Taxi, Sir?" a podgy, Sri Lankan man in a white shirt and smart trousers asked.
"No thank you. I'm looking for the bus to Colombo. Do you know where I can get the bus?"
"3,000 rupees (£15) to Colombo", the taxi man said. "Is a good price."
"No thank you. I want to take the bus."
"Ok Sir, 2,500 rupees. You won't get a better price than that. Ask anyone here." *We seem to be having different conversations. I'll have to be more insistent.* "I want to take the bus, yes?"
"Oh Sir, ha ha, there are no buses from here. You need a taxi and I can take you for 2,500r"
"I really think there are buses to Colombo", I tried again.
"No Sir, no buses from here."

I was tired from my long, sleepless flight but determined to get this bus. It was much cheaper; I won't deny, an attractive attribute to a man of my frugality, but it's also a great way to exist amongst the local culture. As I searched for clues for this bus other taxi drivers befriended me, each one smartly dressed, pleasant in demeanour and outrageous with their lies. "The buses are not safe, Sir. Baggage is stolen all the time."
"It is Saturday, Sir. All bus drivers are on holiday on Saturdays." To be fair, it was a Saturday.
"The bus takes 4 hours, Sir. My taxi is comfortable, quick and has air-conditioning. Only 3,000 rupees, you won't find a better price."

The thought that these taxi drivers are trying to earn an almost honest living help to remain jovial. I could tell a young(ish), white bloke, fresh off the plane and naive to their trickery was a gift from the Gods to this lot.

Eventually an unnecessarily grumpy lady at the transport advice window reluctantly pointed me to a decrepit white and rust shuttle bus that took me to a nearby bus station and a 20-seater, air-conditioned bus that would drive south westerly for an hour to reach Colombo.

A kind young fella in the queue told me it should cost 100r (50p) but upon arrival the conductor gave me 300r change from my 1,000r note. "Hang on, fella." I said, showing him the 300r and raising my eyebrows in expectation. He put another 400r in my hand. *Ahh, go on then yer cheeky monkey.* I put that down as the price of a crash course in the tricks and spills of the locals.

They dropped me off at a thoroughly unpleasant bus station in Colombo full of smog, litter and chaos. There was no way of telling which bus station I was at; I only knew that I needed to go south to Mount Lavinia, that it was bone-meltingly hot, that I was tired, hungry and thirsty and that I was the only traveller in sight.

"Do you know how I can get to Mount Lavinia?" I enquired from a young chap at a food stall and within minutes we were in his tuk tuk on our way. Brilliantly, he knew exactly where my guesthouse was.

In Britain we tell our children that roads are dangerous places but they are, in fact, nurseries compared to Sri Lanka's roads. Galle Road, which runs south parallel to the sea and through Colombo's sprawling districts, is a hectic, multi-lane nightmare of unyielding, anarchic death traps. The road markings split Galle Road into three lanes whilst the traffic splits into five or six (ish). Horns are constant and there appears to be no highway code whatsoever. Everyone rushes all over the road in the attempt to arrive sometime before they set off.

Everyone must have a go in a tuk tuk. It is the most thrilling way of almost killing yourself. For those of you who don't know, a tuk tuk is a three-wheeled blend of a crap motorbike and a crap car. It is almost like a motor bike pulling a chariot. The driver sits centrally in the front with motor bike handles whilst the customers ride in a back seat wide enough to squeeze in three small people. It boasts a bit of zip, is open to the elements and has all the safety features of a skateboard. In the world of motoring tuk tuks are what Blackpool is to theme park rides - the thrill is found in how shoddy it is.

The real magic of the tuk tuk, however, is in the driver. Most drivers will scare you silly as a matter of standard practice but occasionally you get the real big-dipper of drivers. I met one in Bangkok a few years ago. He seemed perfectly placid as we queued in the outside lane on the approach to one of Bangkok's biggest roundabouts wanting to turn right (in Thailand they drive on the left). Suddenly, demonstrating an impressive incapacity for patience, he revved his engine and hopped over the central reservation onto the wrong side of the dual carriageway. We sped to the roundabout, drove the wrong way round it (efficiently bypassing the queue and the longer, legal route round the roundabout), and happily turned right a second before a tsunami of traffic careered into us. In Britain this would be considered "crazy driving" but in Thailand it was a courageous and enterprising piece of initiative.

During our journey down Galle Road I remembered hearing from a Sri Lankan girl I had worked with that Sri Lankans are passionate about two things; their cricket, and their booze! *I wonder if that's true... I'll ask this chap.* "Oh yes, I love cricket", said Sudesh, a chatty man in his mid-twenties who spent his days studying tourism, running his bakeries stall and frightening folk in his tuk tuk. "Everyone in Sri Lanka loves cricket." *That's one for cricket.*

"I was told that Sri Lankan people like drinking too."

"Some people, yes. Some people a lot, but not me really. I don't drink much." *WHAT!? A 'no'! Interesting... I shall have to continue this research into Sri Lanka Sociology. It appears current understanding is somewhat vague.*

My eyes slid shut and my head drooped but another sharp turn startled me awake again. It had been over twenty four hours since I had slept. I kept nodding off for the whole drive but if there's one thing that can keep you awake it's a tuk tuk journey. "Do you have a wife?" Sudesh asked, waking me up again. "What? Err... no", I replied.

"A girlfriend?"

"No", I replied again.

"No?" Sudesh sounded surprised. "Why not?" *Why not? Well... err...*

"Err... I don't know, Sudesh. Do you have a girlfriend?" I asked, too tired to care.

"Not right now, but soon I hope." *Well... grand!*

Sudesh stopped several times to ask strangers where 'Dammika Home' was. *So much for knowing exactly where my guesthouse was.* Eventually we found it down a quiet side street between the bustling Galle Road and the beach. I had chosen it because it was cheap (obviously) and the customer reviews reported Dammika to be friendly and helpful – appealing attributes for the first night of a trip into the unknown.

"Hello, I'm Gavin Anderson", I introduced on my arrival. "I have booked a room for two nights."

"Ah, hello Gavin", Dammika welcomed enthusiastically. "Yes, I'm expecting you, come in. Don't worry about your shoes. I'll show you your room. You will want a shower of course and then I can tell you about Colombo." Dammika was a spritely, young, 60 year old Sri Lankan who welcomed me into his home with all the warmth he could muster.

Once I'd showered and slept for five hours I listened to Dammika's tirade of information about the local amenities. He vehemently insisted I get a sim card and told me the best place to buy one. He explained where the supermarket was, where I could buy beer, where I could eat out, what bus to get into Colombo, that a taxi to the airport should be 2,000r and a tuk tuk into Colombo centre should be 400r. It turns out the 900r I paid Sudesh was considerably over the odds. *This price I'm paying for learning the tricks is growing excessively.*

Dammika helpfully suggested three or four places for dinner and I found exactly none of them. Instead, I visited The Lion Bar a little further down Galle Road; a restaurant / bar selling barbequed food. My first night in Sri Lanka was an occasion that should be marked with a hearty meal and a couple of easy beers – Lion beer as it turned out.

I nibbled away my barbeque chicken and sipped at my cold Lion beer in the pleasant evening warmth of the spacious outside courtyard. My mind wandered, imagining exotic adventures and Test Cricket before being drawn back to reality by nine young Sri Lankan gents at the next table who had drunk just enough Lion beer to begin gently singing Ronan Keating's 'When you say nothing at all'. It was a curious song choice for a bunch of young Sri Lankan men, not just for the geographical and cultural difference but that song was released by Ronan Keating back in 1999 (and originally released in 1988). Curious too how softly and heartfelt they sang it.

This courageous display of public singing reminded me of my Welsh singing friend, Arfon, who also enjoys an impromptu sing-song after a few beers. Arfon is 55 and spent his younger days travelling, working and singing his way round the world and though he's now more settled that young adventurer lives on and so too does his compulsion to sing.

He'll regularly burst into song in pubs, streets, restaurants – anywhere really. When a taxi driver asked "where to" Arfon replied with a rendition of Simon and Garfunkel's 'Homeward Bound'.

Despite being proudly Welsh his signature tune is that Irish classic, 'The Wild Rover', and he'll happily sing all four verses. In a swish Italian restaurant a talented Italian pianist luckily remembered how to play it and startled customers were treated to two verses and two choruses of Arfon's old favourite, thanking him with thunderous applause (except for our work colleagues sitting aghast in the corner).

Arfon's proudest public-singing accomplishment, however, was on a return train journey from a drinking visit to North Yorkshire where he led the whole carriage in singing The Wild Rover. He continued with a few more classics much to the delight of the old train conductor who, at the end of the line, shook Arfon's hand saying "This has been the best night of my life." Let's hope not... if only for the sake of Mrs Train Conductor, but a terrific effort nonetheless.

Now midnight, the nine fellas at the next table had moved boisterously up the gears and onto Aswad (???) and other songs not released in the last 10 years. *Where do they get their music from?* One fella in particular was having a gallant, though ultimately unsuccessful, attempt at vocal harmonies. *He's my favourite.*

Their grand finale was 'Sweet Chariot' and they smashed it home with nothing more than guts and enthusiasm, especially my favourite chap who continued his attempts at harmonies. *If this is what I can expect from Sri Lankans this trip will be a glorious success.* On that last off-note they staggered out giving me a wave as they went - I think they caught me singing along to 'Leaving on a Jet Plane'.

So that was, I presumed, a typical first taste of Sri Lanka. The only thing left to do was to suffer sleep deprivation torture from the heat despite the ceiling fan making an appreciated contribution. Fifteen minutes after a cold shower I had another one. After eventually falling asleep I woke up halfway through the night in a roasting oven Dammika pretended was a bedroom... and the fan was off. *What is the meaning of this!?* I tried the switch but nothing happened. I tried the light switch but nothing happened. *Blast! A power cut.* I had another cold shower and suffered some more.

Chapter 3 – Colombo (Part 1)

Dammika's guesthouse centred on a roomy and comfortable combined lounge and dining area with a small kitchen at the back and a porch at the front. He had three or four basic but spacious en-suite rooms available for 2,000r to 2,500r (£10 to £12.50). The porch looked out onto a small but neat garden and driveway surrounded by high stone walls. A young-looking Sri Lankan lady hovered about cleaning and cooking if Dammika had his way. Otherwise she spent great slabs of time watching TV soaps.

After breakfast Dammika made two enthusiastic introductions. The first was to an old Swiss bloke, well-educated, well-travelled and Dammika's boss from his days working for the Red Cross. He was enjoying a small holiday touring Sri Lanka and had stopped off to see his old buddy, Dammika.

The second was to a bottle of the local tipple, Old Arrack. It was a whisky made from the bark of a coconut tree that Dammika recommended drinking as often as possible with soda or lemonade. A tad unorthodox, perhaps, to start drinking whisky at 10:30am but this trip was never about the orthodox.

The first went down nicely and Dammika soon began to handle the bottle once again. "Only a little bit for me, Dammika", said the Swiss boss as Dammika ignored him completely. Clearly such protests were ineffective so I didn't bother.

Dammika, now about 60, had started work in the Merchant Navy at the age of 18 as the Ship Radiographer (well before the days of the internet and satellite navigation) and continued for 20 years. A Radiographer's typical day, he told me, would start at 8am checking for telegrams received and informing the necessary people of any communications. At midday he would report the ship's position to Head Office before starting work on some beers. At 16:30 he would check again for telegrams and help any crew members speak with their families and friends. The radiographing day finished at 18:30 upon which he would return to the urgent business of those beers.

It was a sailor's life for Dammika and it had taken him all over the world. Whenever I asked him if he'd been somewhere he always waggled his head and replied "Yes, of course. I've been everywhere."

When the ship was in port Dammika was off duty. By law the radio room was locked and Dammika was free to explore the exotic places in which he found himself. Like any typical sailing crew they earned their money at sea and blew it on wild parties at port. Somewhere along the line he met his wife who, unsurprisingly, urged him to consider that the sailor' life wasn't for him and that he should stay in Sri Lanka to help raise a family.

And so he sold his radiographing services to the Swiss Red Cross and his Swiss boss whom he was currently plying with Old Arrack. The Swiss Red Cross were in Sri Lanka giving help and support to those who needed it courtesy of the Sri Lankan Civil War. When the war eventually ended in 2009 the Red Cross, and Dammika's involvement in it, were no longer needed. In December 2011, Dammika opened 'Dammika Home' to accommodate paying guests whom he tries to get drunk before noon.

After just three months of business Dammika was proud to announce he'd had visitors from thirty four different countries and his rooms were full virtually every day, probably because his rooms were the cheapest that the most diligent of shoppers could find. These days he meets and greets people from all over the world, seldom wears a shirt and continues to operate a radio.

Dammika, it turns out, was the President of Sri Lanka's Radiology Group. His radio is always set up and ready to use, still holding faith in this old, reliable technology. It came in useful during the tsunami disaster of 2004 when all other forms of communication were down. "When satellites stop working, and internet stops working, radio will still work", he told me. John Maclean in Die Hard 4.0 expressed the same view.

If I had planned the day I would not have drunk any of the local whisky and seen lots of Colombo. As it was I drank lots of the local whisky and saw none of Colombo. This was not the exploratory start to this trip I'd had in mind (and I was due to move on somewhere (???) the following day). However, I doubt I could have had a more welcoming introduction to Sri Lanka. The main sights of Colombo had to wait for another day, but I thought I should at least venture out of Dammika's Saloon and go for a stroll.

Donning my flip flops I walked along the quiet backstreets occupied only by a few scraggy dogs looking for scraps of food or something to have sex with. After only 300 yards I was at the beach; a dirty, messy and disagreeable area spoiled by the city perhaps. Looking left (south) down the beach I could see the bright white walls of the exclusively posh Mount Lavinia Hotel and in the opposite direction, in the distance, stood the tall buildings of Colombo city centre.

The most common sight on the beach was young couples canoodling; sometimes walking along the beach, sometimes sat on benches, sometimes sat on the sand, always under umbrellas. *Umbrellas!?* I looked up; the sky was a perfect sheet of blue. *What the hell's going on?* Sometimes women walked alone with an umbrella; sometimes two or three under one umbrella. Fellas, though, only ever had an umbrella if they were escorting their good lady. *Hmmm…*

A little further down the beach a few local teenagers were splashing around in the sea, climbing over a small wooden boat. I couldn't tell if they were playing or fishing. "Hey!" one serious looking chap said approaching me. "Which country?"
"I'm sorry?"
"Which country?" he repeated, sternly.
"What? Where I come from?"
"Yes."
"I'm from England." I said, smiling.
"You should give them some money." He instructed.
"Pardon? What do you mean?"
"They are trying to fish but haven't caught anything. They are hungry. You have to give me money so I can help them buy food." He instructed again with a serious look on his face.
"You want money from me?" I asked, for confirmation.
"Of course. They are very poor." *Hmmm. What's the right thing to do here? Is it desperation? Is it a scam? Are these kids starving? This lad is a little aggressive … I know…*
"I'm not giving you any money, fella. And stop following me!" I said, flatly. Well… I didn't like the cut of his jib.

My flip flops, under-worn over the past year in the unsuitable climes of Sheffield, had made my feet sore so I turned off to find Galle Road again and wander back via the supermarket Dammika had pointed out to buy some pens.

Stood between the supermarket and me was the brutal wall of unrelenting ferocity that is Galle Road. Like the Great Walls of Troy it presented a commanding barrier. I was in need of a wooden horse filled with deceitful, murderous Greeks! I watched a fella try to cross with a better chance of passing through a herd of charging wildebeest on their annual migration and yet I stood bedazzled as he stepped out and smoothly floated through the mad scramble of traffic with ease, clearly trained in some form of dark magic. That he managed it without any stress or anxiety on his face at all amazed me no less than if I'd seen him walk on water.

The Municipal Council of Colombo had thoughtfully sought to help by providing a zebra crossing that the road users were ignoring and the pedestrians were, in understandable response, not using. This zebra crossing proved just as useful to no one as any of the other road markings. In order to not help people further the Council had provided regular zebra crossings up and down Galle Road resulting in the road users ignoring more zebra crossings and the pedestrians not using more zebra crossings. By the time of my approach more zebra crossings on Galle Road were not being used than ever before.

I stood for five minutes watching other people cross this seemingly un-fordable torrent with enviable grace. *How has he done that? Where was the gap? How has she done that? And why has she got an umbrella!?*

The answer is that this 10-lane horror, although monstrous, wasn't as savage as it originally made out; it just required a little courage. I stepped off the sanctity of the pavement and into the cauldron of danger - an actual leap of faith. Gradually and tentatively I edged across the road.

To my intense joy the great tide of traffic flowed around me as naturally as wading through a flowing stream. We were in complete accord. This powerful animal was wild but also forgiving and flexible; not the ever-flowing Trojan Wall of steel it appeared to be. To paraphrase Professor Dumbledore, *Galle Road will always provide help to those who ask for it,* although I fear for any Sri Lankan who attempts this technique in Britain!

As an added bonus I realised that the women carried umbrellas to shield themselves from the sun; an entirely alien concept to a pale Brit like me. In my 33 years of life in England I have never once seen anyone walk down the street with an umbrella on a hot, sunny day. It has probably never occurred. It transpires that where we white folk like to get a tan, Asian folk like to avoid one. *A beautification reason – I should have known.*

I carried a 3-pack of biros to the checkout and saw Alistair Cook, England's opening batsman, achieve his 3rd century of the year in a one day international against Pakistan. The supermarket, with some stroke of genius I might add, had hung a TV monitor above the checkout showing the cricket to enhance the customers' queuing experience immeasurably. *The Sri Lankans must really love their cricket to prompt such investment from supermarket management.*

I can only conclude that sales drop considerably whenever the cricket is on. Sri Lankans everywhere remain camped in their front rooms unwilling to leave the cricket even for the 30 minutes to pick up the groceries. The result is cricket in the Sri Lankan supermarket and moaning about check-out queues is a pastime reserved for western, cricket-less shoppers. There were people still stood there after they'd paid for their shopping. *Utterly brilliant!*

With a couple of beers and a bottle of Old Arrack I shared a magnificent dinner of rice and curry that Dammika's wife had kindly cooked for us all.

"Dammika, what do Sri Lankans mainly eat?" I asked.

"Rice and curry", he replied.

"All the time?" I asked again.

"Yes, all the time."

"I see", I said, considering this. "And what is the usual Sri Lankan breakfast?"

"Rice and curry."

"The Thai girls charge 2,000 baht!?" Dammika exclaimed astounded. "That's terrible. It used to be only 200 baht!"

"200 baht!? Really?" Whilst Dammika was generously pouring the Old Arrack I explained my plans to travel to Thailand, Laos, Cambodia and Vietnam. "Have you ever been to Thailand, Dammika?" I had asked.

"Yes, of course. I've been everywhere." He replied. "Lots of girls and happy times there, but they always make you pay for it. Some countries, the girls would come to the boat and bang on the side because they want to party, they want a good time. Other countries, like Thailand, they did the same but they were poor so they ask for money."

I knew exactly what he was talking about. When I was in Phuket 5 years previous my friend and I were walking down the street on our way to Rock City Nightclub when a Thai girl, carrying her groceries and dressed in her waitress garb, tripped over in front of us. In my best Thai I asked if she was alright. She smiled as I picked her up and we chatted as we walked on. She was a delightful girl, happy-go-lucky, pretty and funny - I invited her to join us to Rock City (under the pretence to celebrate National Rock Day) and happily she did, along with 3 barmaids we met at her local. "How did that happen?" I asked my mate.

"I dunno," he replied with a big grin on his face, "but four girls are better than one."

We drank and danced and kissed – things were going splendidly. Eventually I asked her if she'd like to come to my hotel and she started giggling. *What the hell does that mean?* I thought, embarrassed. Still half giggling she said she would like to but I would need to give her 2,000baht. *2,000baht!?* I declined.

By the end of the evening Dammika had asked whether I had a girlfriend, we had talked of being a sailor, the stock markets, the civil war and quite possibly many other things, and I knew Dammika loved his booze. Just to be complete with my research I asked if he loved his cricket too. Of course he did.

"The best way to get into the city centre is on the train", Dammika explained in the morning. "There is a train station close to here and it will take you to Fort and Maradana." 'Fort' is Colombo's main train station in the centre of the city and the Maradana district, with its Sri Lankan Department of Immigration, was my destination. I was off to extend my visa to the full 90 days to allow me back into Sri Lanka after visiting Indochina. "Oh, great. How do I find the train station?" I asked.
"It is easy. Go out of the house and turn left, walk down the street towards the beach and turn right."
"Great. Oh, how do I know when to turn right?" I enquired further.
"You will be standing on the train track." *Of course. Silly me.* I bid Dammika a good morning and headed out.

I decided that Dammika was right; it would be useful to have a local mobile phone if only for calling ahead to guesthouses so I stopped off at 'Dialogue'. For only 800r (£4) I received a sim card and extra phone credit that all failed to work on my bloody phone! It was "locked", apparently, and I would need another one. *Blast! I'll buy a cheap, rubbish phone in Maradana.*

"Hello, I'm looking for a cheap, rubbish phone for my new Dialogue sim card", I began at a small phone stall I found on arrival in Maradana.

"Ok, Sir. What kind of phone?" said the relaxed middle-aged stall-keeper.
"A cheap one."
"Cheap?" he asked
"Cheap!"
"What about this one, sir, this is a good phone." The stall keeper handed me a packaged phone.
"Oh, it is good isn't it," I observed, "but, perhaps, a cheaper one?"
"Cheaper?" he asked.
"Cheapest!" I said.
"Cheapest?"
"Cheapest!"
"Well, what about this one, Sir. This is cheap."
"Ah yes, is this your cheapest phone?"
"Yes Sir."
I smiled and said "Perfect!"

This rubbish phone was 3,000r (£15) and rubbish. It had a technologically ancient screen with graphics in two colours, black and a kind of beige/green. There were none of those advanced smart phone features or internet capability. More importantly, this rubbish phone was brilliant! I could call and text people, it had an alarm, a clock and a torch – all the fundamental requirements of a traveller. Furthermore, its battery went on forever and it was brilliantly simple to use - there were none of those advanced smart phone features or internet capability.

I walked towards the Sri Lankan Department of Immigration, along some of central Colombo's main roads, amongst the local hustle and bustle of everyday Sri Lankan activity. This was it – *real Sri Lanka*. In amongst the people, witnessing a culture far different from my own; being in a place where people live their lives completely differently.

Many Sri Lankan blokes walked around barefoot. *Well, why not. Let the feet breathe.* And they all wore trousers... smart trousers. I was the only person wearing shorts (apart from Dammika but I was beginning to think him a bit unorthodox). *Why is this? Protection from the sun again? To maintain a smart appearance, perhaps? I'd be roasting in trousers.* My third puzzlement was that every now and then someone would spit some red stuff on the floor - wholly peculiar behaviour to my mind.

In my pre-occupation of pondering these mind-blowing cultural differences I had gotten myself completely lost and required the services of a knowledgeable tuk tuk driver.

With an enormous slice of luck I found a young, excitable tuk tuk driver. The young ones are often the best. Their thrill for adventure and eagerness to complete journeys quickly has not yet been eroded over time. I was carried spritely towards the Sri Lankan Department of Immigration and in doing so I acquired an inkling into the minds of the local road users. There is a highway code in effect on these streets after all. It is simple, effective, fair and consists of one simple rule:

If there is a space somewhere, you can take it.

That was it, and in heavy traffic it helps to be small. The tuk tuk slips into tiny spaces ahead of cars, trucks and buses. That's fair game and tolerated as such. There are no such things as queues or right of way. If there's a space, you can take it.

Also, the horns are not used as a show of annoyance. "HONNNKKKKK" doesn't mean "you cut me up, you bastard" like it does in Britain, or to inform someone they're driving crazily. Instead it means "watch out, fella! I'm here and I'm coming through," or, "Hello. I'm about to drive crazily." It is to ensure they are seen BEFORE they drive crazily. That way, other road users can take evasive action in anticipation of crazy driving occurring.

There seems little point in honking retrospectively to say "you were just driving crazily there, fella!" They probably already know. Paradoxically, if a car is able to honk then they have no doubt already survived the crazy driving rendering the honking redundant. You would only need to honk retrospectively if the danger turned out to be real and one or both cars lie crashed in a ditch. On reflection, Sri Lanka's system seems wholly more effective and considerate than ours.

Finally, I reached the Sri Lankan Department of Immigration. *Thank God!* Unfortunately when I thanked God for my deliverance I was quite unaware that it was in fact the Devil that had arranged this meeting.

If you were to imagine a hell where anything remotely exciting, interesting or fun had been removed completely and time slowed to a pace next to 'stop' without actually, and regrettably, being 'stop', you will be imagining Sri Lanka's Department of Immigration. It was a joyless place - bereft of character, humour, hope and, very nearly, me and my visa extension application. In place of these things flourished bureaucracy, red tape, forms, procedure and an overwhelming feeling of dullness. I'm quite sure this bleak picture I have painted is not nearly bleak enough.

Miserable grey walls surrounded rows of seats that were provided for us to sit on whilst marvelling at the miserable grey walls. These walls were in fact partitions, on the other side of which unhurried officials administered the extension of people's visas.

If you like a good queue you'd love the Department of Immigration. It's full of queues and all of them are real belters! Queue enthusiasts would revel in the realisation that participants must have a go on all queues once they've deduced in which order they are to be enjoyed. Some queues were physical where its participants stood in a line or crowded round a desk. Some queues were intangible, ordered by a number system, and there were queues that were hybrids of those queues. You could sometimes be in a queue completely unaware of the system, the rules or whether you were actually in a queue at all. And you may find yourself in two or more queues at once.

I had forgotten my passport photos which gave me the opportunity to join three more queues, one of which was an entirely fake queue with no purpose at all. Whilst I queued for a visa extension form a young, tall and stocky Sri Lankan chap in a red Adidas cap asked me, in fine English, if he could borrow my pen. Half an hour later, whilst standing in a queue acclaimed for its sheer length and inconsistency of speed I felt a tap on the shoulder and the young lad in the red Adidas cap returned my pen. That brief exchange was regarded as a glimmer of interest in an otherwise desolate and baron afternoon.

The participants of the long and inconsistent queue would eventually be interviewed by an Immigration Official who was, no doubt, well-trained and thorough in applying Immigration scrutiny. "So, Mr Anderson, you want a visa extension?"
"Yes please", I replied.
"Ok."

The officials, in the most part, were very official and professional. Despite the hordes of people pouring in the staff were phased not a jot! Smartly dressed, unhurried officials ambled leisurely behind the partitions carrying baskets of passports across the room or hovering over more important, less hurried officials leisurely completing paperwork.

Not one of these steadfast and professional officials allowed the pressure to get to them. Even when the need for administrative activity was at its most urgent they remained calm and unperturbed. I'm quite sure many-a-visitor would have walked out mid-process and spent the rest of the day drinking themselves back to sanity if the Department of Immigration didn't have hold of their passport and I'm quite sure the Department of Immigration knew it.

Clearly in need of some conversation to occupy his mind the chap in the red Adidas cap came to sit next to me. It was reassuring to know that one's company is preferential to these glum, grey walls. 'Red cap's' name was Kish, a man in his early twenties. Having been born and raised in Sri Lanka he now lives in London and works for Orange. He told me how his family sold their nice house in the hill country raising some £18,000 to send Kish to Thames Valley and Kingston University. When Kish moved to London four and a half years ago his family moved to the Southern Coast city of Galle.

This was Kish's first visit back to Sri Lanka since then and The Department of Immigration welcomed him back by charging the maximum visa extension of £30, the cost of a 60 day extension, for just the 6 days he required.

Chatting to Kish provided some welcome entertainment for the both of us as we watched everyone else have their passports returned. Kish asked me if I had a girlfriend. *Good God! Is everyone in Sri Lanka interested in that?* It appears they are. We established that not only did I not have a girlfriend, Kish didn't have a girlfriend either.

Kish was a nice fella, and slightly nervous which made his effort and eagerness to talk to a stranger such as me all the more admirable. He was keenly interested in my travel plans, though in this room one could be keenly interested in a stain on the carpet. He was especially happy to learn that I would soon be in Galle to watch the cricket at the same time as he would be. We swapped phone numbers and promised to meet up.

It was the final furlong. Once I had paid I queued (whilst sat down and close to death waiting to hear my name be called out) to collect my passport from the front desk again. After that I was finally released from this torturous nightmare having been driven near insane and realised that only 5 hours had passed on the outside world whilst I had suffered for half a lifetime.

Thrilled to have The Department of Immigration at my stern I rushed through Fort station where a bloke spat some red stuff on to the platform and a kind gent helped me to buy a ticket.

Dammika wasn't home when I arrived to pick up my bags but his youngish helper was in the garden watering the plants and her mouth with a hose. As I explained to her in simple English that I had to leave right away to catch my train to Kandy she occasionally spat bright red water onto the lawn. *What the hell is going on!? Is that the same red stuff?* Sadly this mystery had to wait – I was running late for my train!

Chapter 4 – Around Kandy

Have you ever stood on a train platform looking at the opposite platform thinking, *I could just walk across the track to get there? It would be much easier than walking up and down that bridge.* I have, lots of times, but I had never done it for fear of being branded 'a lunatic' and thrown out of the station. In Fort Station, however, this practice was commonplace. No one was a lunatic or branded as such. The train track is for everyone and it is understood that it is really not overly-tricky to avoid getting hit by a train. I was very pleased to be given the opportunity.

Although I was beginning to learn bits and pieces of how to get about in Sri Lanka every experience was new and alien. On the evening train to Kandy I felt unnerved and naïve. Each carriage was full as Sri Lankan commuters squeezed into the central aisles. I was the only backpacker on board; a bumbling, clueless white man sticking up head and shoulders out of a sea of shorter, street-wise locals. My backpack had barged its way through the crowd, occupied valuable space and half-blocked the way for peddlers traipsing through the carriages selling drinks, chicken, egg rolls, fruit and various completely unrecognisable things. I felt guilty and unwelcome. Occasionally I made eye contact with another passenger and smiled in the hope of causing no offence. No smiles were returned.

After half an hour the train began to slow and a man sitting close to me stood up and offered me his seat. Embarrassed, I politely declined – there were many others he could have offered it to. The lady in the adjacent seat urged me to take the seat which I politely declined again but she insisted.

A middle-aged man eventually took her seat and quickly demonstrated a keen interest in my Lonely Planet book. His English wasn't great and the noise from the train was. He seemed to enthusiastically divulge an encyclopaedic amount of amazing local facts and anecdotes with magical wonder in his eyes and I didn't grasp a word of it.

During his undeservingly wasted enlightenments he paused a moment to offer to buy me a quartered apple with chilli and salt sprinkled on it from one of the peddlers. I politely declined, a decision he chose to ignore entirely and bought me a quartered apple with chilli and salt sprinkled on it.

The act of buying a snack for an out-of–town stranger on the commute home struck me as a special generosity and the act of doing so, even though I didn't want it, struck me as slightly peculiar. More peculiar, of course, is the act of sprinkling chilli and salt on your apple and the taste of it, though not unpleasant, more peculiar still. The most surprising aspect of this small nugget of bewilderment was that this apple was delivered in a home-made paper bag constructed from a school child's maths homework. Customers here receive a free lesson with their snacks. *How ingenious.*

My friendly co-passenger was Krishanthe and, bless his cotton socks, he had made me feel much more welcome. Before leaving the train he gave me his email address, phone number and a pledge of assistance should I encounter any problems in Sri Lanka. I had good reason to believe him too. He had already assisted me with problems I didn't have, as well as the apple, by phoning ahead to my guesthouse in Kandy to make sure everything was alright.

I was greeted at the guesthouse by an aggressive Alsatian and the well reputed and much-loved dear old Mrs Clement Dissanayake who unsympathetically told me to go somewhere else. My train had arrived late and Vinon the tuk tuk driver had driven me to Mrs Clement's house at 10:30pm so I could blunder into her life and get her out of bed. Despite Krishanthe phoning ahead, Mrs Clement had given my room away but, not totally without conscience, had reserved a room in a guesthouse nearby for my first night.

In the morning, just as we hadn't agreed, Vinon picked me up at 7:30am from the gates of Mrs Clement's guesthouse. I had dumped my backpack in her house some 30 minutes earlier and Vinon blamed the Kandian rush-hour traffic for his tardiness.

My plan for the day was to follow Vinon's plan. He had offered to take me on a jaunt jam-packed with the main highlights of the Kandian hill-country for 3,000r (£15). Having seen none of the orthodox sights of Colombo Vinon's offer was well-timed.

Though most Sri Lankan gents were skinny, Vinon was a healthy fella; a young-looking, thirty-one year old family man with just enough sales patter to win him some fares. Vinon was a tuk tuk driver of rare sensibility. I kept hoping he might treat me to some adventuresome driving but he remained placid. Occasionally he threatened to overtake a dawdling old van or a dangerously laden scooter but, instead, meekly settled into formation behind it.

He took great pride in keeping his tuk tuk clean and in good repair and delighted in telling me of its superior power and specification without ever demonstrating this capability. We cruised the Sri Lankan country lanes on our way to the Elephant Orphanage, making just the one stop for Vinon to buy a new tuk tuk carpet!

The well-recommended Pinnewala Elephant Orphanage charged 2,000r (£10) entry and Vinon got in for free. The ninety or so elephants wandered around a few acres of sloping, stinking field apart from a big old blind elephant that was chained up presumably so he didn't bungle about hurting anyone.

Visitors were free to roam the top of the hill where some elephants came close enough to touch although, rather importantly, the movement of the randy, young male elephants was restricted in case they developed the mood for a mighty display of strength and aggression. Boys will be boys.

"We should go down to the main street now to get the best view," Vinon advised, having been here hundreds of times before. "What do you mean, Vinon? The best view of what?"

He stationed us at the main entrance to enjoy the magnificent view of eighty elephants hurtling toward us. I took refuge behind a stone gatepost as they eagerly bounded across the main road (without argument from the traffic) and rumbled down the street towards the river. It is a bizarre thing to watch eighty elephants march down a street lined with shops and bars but here it happens twice a day.

This wide river is the highlight of these elephants' life. The grown-ups cool down and relax, the young ones play, and the ones in between either try to hump something, or try not to get humped; a game played the world over.

Tourists climbed over the rocks stretching into the river, getting close to the elephants to take their photos. Often, a young elephant's curiosity drew them to the eager tourists and only rarely did the mahouts step in to curb their progress. "Urhkurkh!" "Urhkurkh!" they shouted, which I understand means 'back off and behave yourself'. If I had wanted to I could have waded through the river amongst the elephants and their frolicking. *You wouldn't be able to do that at Chester Zoo.*

"Hey, Sir. You want photo… with baby?" I heard. I turned and saw two mahouts smiling and nodding. "Yeah! Great!" They led me away from the main crowd and behind a huge rock where a juvenile elephant was busily investigating this stretch of river. "Closer, closer", one of them urged, snapping away with my camera. *I bet you can't do this at Chester Zoo either.* I did as he had bid and cuddled this wonderful, young elephant wondering what he was thinking about the whole thing. On returning my camera the mahout said, "Could you please help... the mahouts? We are not paid well", he pleaded. "We need help to support our families."

Ahhh, it's a scam! The devious little critters with their sneaky operation behind this big rock - it was brilliant! I admire any scam that involves concealing an elephant. I gave the fellas a bit of money if only for their creativity and boldness. *They definitely don't do this at Chester Zoo!*

One of the shops on the street to the river sells paper made entirely from elephant dung. Every time the herd of elephants walked up and down this street they deposited 'raw materials' from which this shop made a variety of paper products. If necessity is the mother of invention, what on Earth was necessary to invent elephant dung paper? I felt it necessary to send some elephant dung to my brother in the form of a birthday card. *Happy Birthday, Bro!!*

After a mildly interesting tour of a tea factory Vinon and I enjoyed a free cup of sweet tea in their cafe. "Rsschnnss", Vinon muttered, leaning in with narrow eyes.
"Sorry, what?" Vinon leaned in closer and muttered "Russians" before jerking his head over his shoulder and screwing up his face in disapproval. Kandy receives plenty of Russians, I discovered, and Vinon doesn't like any of them. "Russian... Russian... Russian..." he whispered discreetly pointing round the café but I thought better of inviting him to elaborate. In return Vinon discovered that I didn't have a girlfriend and with that it was time to move swiftly on to the idyllic Peradeniya Botanical Garden.

This Botanical Garden contains 147 acres of astonishingly varied and immaculately kept flora to delight any plant and garden enthusiast. For the keen botanist it is so vast a place to explore we might be able to put Alan Titchmarsh in there and never hear from him again.

Of particular repute and botanical interest is their impressive collection of orchids but there is also the spice house, the bamboo forest, the medicinal garden and, extraordinarily, an extensive collection of grasses. For the visitor like me, more interested in the aesthetically pleasing nature of the gardens than any particular scientific relevance, it is a wonderfully peaceful place to relax and casually explore.

Wandering around these gardens reminded me of my friend, Tash. Tash, by way of a brief introduction, is a thoughtful, intelligent, funny, socially conscious, dirty, horrible little bastard. He is a man of extremes and a walking paradox. He is somehow both fat and skinny at the same time and has been described as the most stupid, intelligent man one could meet, *or was it the most intelligent, stupid man?* He displays an abundance of confidence whilst suffering from gut-wrenching pangs of self-guilt. He is the most charming, witty, insightful company you could hope for, and utterly filthy, offensive and inappropriate. I can only imagine that to be torn so vigorously in opposing directions is a constant torture. He has somehow managed to arrange his finances so that he is both wealthy and skint, and approaches healthy living with staunch motivation whilst enthusiastically obliterating himself regularly. He is, quite incredibly, all of this simultaneously.

One of Tash's exploratory habits is to spot hidden niches where one could take one's girlfriend for secret outdoor sex. "That'd be a good place to sneak off with the missus", he'd say with glee, making a mental note of its location should he ever go back with a future girlfriend. "So would that". He has a natural gift for it. I can tell you that Croatia's Plitvice lakes are riddled with potential secret sex dens.

So too, it would seem, is Peradeniya Botanical Gardens. Dozens of young Sri Lankan couples had half-secluded themselves in dozens of nooky holes and were canoodling in bushes, behind trees, round corners and almost exclusively under umbrellas. *The randy little toe-rags.* I was told that a lot of young adults still live in the family home so it was a constant challenge to find a bit of privacy with the girlfriend or boyfriend.

I ambled along Cook's Pine Avenue past a troupe of monkeys and towards a faint but busy squawking noise. The sound, getting louder and louder, came from something in the trees. What first appeared to be a tree full of birds revealed itself to be hundreds... thousands... of large fruit bats roosting upside down. As I reached them I discovered them filling the tops of more and more trees. Occasionally one jerkily flitted from one tree to another amidst the incessant cacophonous squawking which, from a bunch of nocturnal creatures, had no place in the middle of the day!

Next stop - Bahirawakanda Hill (Gnome Mountain), which overlooks Kandy and is a place of great legend; The Legend of the Gnome:-

A terrifying noise was oft heard from the top of the mountain which the people of old Kandy considered to be an evil Gnome calling for a sacrifice to satisfy his appetite for human flesh. Under advice from his minister the King of Kandy sent a beautiful virgin up the mountain every year in accordance with the evil Gnome's demands. One year, the minister's own son's girlfriend was chosen to be sacrificed to the Gnome and, as was customary, she was escorted up the mountain at night and left there. The Gnome was evil indeed and, it transpired, was the Kings own minister. The minister's son, unaware of his Father's damnable ruse, secretly scaled the mountain, defeated the Gnome (his Dad) and rescued his girlfriend from his monstrous clutches. The couple immediately eloped to Colombo only to return years later after the British had taken over.

Now the mountain is adorned with a Buddhist temple and a giant, white Buddha statue sitting atop its roof enjoying the splendid view over Kandy. Visitors too can appreciate the view from the temple or climb a staircase attached to the Buddha's back to get higher but the Buddha itself then blocks the view.

With a bit of effortful manoeuvring over the railings, however, it is possible to climb onto the Buddha's left knee allowing the climber to enjoy a sublime view of Kandy and the Big White Buddha's hospitality.

It occurred to me later that it might be considered offensive to climb onto the Buddha's left knee so on the way back into Kandy I asked Vinon if, hypothetically, climbing onto either of the Buddha's knees would cause offence. He said, hypothetically, that it probably would.

Traditional Kandian dancing is well known throughout Sri Lanka and struck me as a bizarre affair. The show Vinon took me to lasts for an hour with nine or ten different pieces, costing 500r (£2.50). The theatre by the lake in central Kandy resembled a school hall with the raised stage at the front and folding chairs organised into rows. The dancing troupe was finely garbed in traditional Kandian regalia; loose, colourful garments with bells, tassels and, for the lucky ones, a silly hat. The performers consisted of three separate groups, the drummers, the boys and the girls.

Five drummers provided constant rhythm, four of whom looked like they didn't want to be there and the fifth, possibly approaching eighty five, probably shouldn't have been. There were six boys; four were slender, athletic chaps and two were of a more robust construction (they were my favourite). There were also six girls, one of which caught my eye early on. Although she was the best and most attractive of the girl dancers she was stuck out to the side. The central lead girl wasn't nearly as good which might, I pondered, lead a cynical man to conclude that she was having it away with the Production Director.

This was not what you would call a spectacular dancing demonstration though there were a few glimmers of excitement. Two semi-naked fellas jumped on stage, wearing masks of hairy, senile old men and erratically jumped about the stage waving their arms and banging their sticks on the stage to an energetic drum beat. I could see no particular reason behind this commotion but senile old men don't often suffer reason.

Then, in a most surprising turn of events, the geriatric drummer, having already surprised the audience by lasting this long, performed a rocking drum solo that lifted the energy of the whole theatre. No one could understand how he could possibly muster the physical effort.

With the audience freshly energised the only thing left to do was for the boys to bring home the finale with a dance designed for the young men of old Kandy to show off their athletic prowess. Essentially it was a backflip-off. Three of the athletic dancers performed a series of backflips across the stage with increasing difficulty whilst the two chubbier fellas looked on, pleased to sit this one out by the looks of them. The most impressive dancer finished the show with a tumble across the stage of some seven backflips and a somersault to a gladly-received mediocre applause. The audience left feeling entirely justified in paying the £2.50 entrance fee.

Kandy is the Capital of the hill country; rich in history, spiritualism and culture and completely bereft of nightlife. At only 9pm, when me and the rest of the world might want to check out a bar or two before retiring back to Mrs Clement's, there was almost none. The city centre was dark, quiet and empty with only a rare, lonely soul and stray dogs walking the streets.

I decided to walk the long walk to Mrs Clement's, the highlight of which was a chocolate éclair bought from one of Kandy's most prestigious restaurants just before it closed. The lowlight was either getting lost on the long and pointless walk in the wrong direction, the tedious walk back again or the drug dealer who persuaded me to share a tuk tuk with him. "I'm going to the next village", he said. "You're guesthouse is on the way. We can share." *Sure, why not.*

By the time I got there it was 10:30pm and my constant refusal to buy his drugs, once he'd revealed that aspect of his character, moved him to the point of aggression. "You should give me three hundred rupee. For helping you", he argued.

"Helping me!?" I contested. "You've hassled me!" Somewhat distressed I stopped the tuk tuk some way short of Mrs Cement's house, paid the driver and briskly walked away.

I was once again greeted at the guesthouse by the aggressive Alsatian and a slightly miffed dear old Mrs Clement Dissanayake whom I'd once again roused out of bed.

After that I still felt I was in the unknown, not knowing how to operate, not knowing how things worked and not understanding the people. Vinon had looked after me but the evening's befuddlement with the drug dealer had knocked my confidence and spirits. I felt dependant… vulnerable. *And I must stop getting Mrs Clement out of bed!!*

Chapter 5 – Kandy

Kandy (population 110,000) is one of Sri Lanka's major cities but is still only one twentieth the size of Colombo. Its most notable physical feature is a large man-made lake that sprawls easterly from the city centre with a small island that a former ruler of Kandy used to house his personal harem. When the British arrived in Kandy, clearly favouring war to sex, they turned the island into an ammunitions store.

At the side of the lake sits Kandy's chief cultural attraction, The Temple of the Sacred Tooth Relic, a grand, white temple that they say houses the tooth of Buddha. Legend says the Buddha's tooth was snatched out of the flames of his funeral pyre in 483BC and later smuggled into Sri Lanka when no one was looking. Since then Sri Lankans have believed that whoever holds the tooth shall rule Sri Lanka.

Conspiracy theories question the validity of the tooth suggesting the item currently in Kandy is a replica and the original was destroyed by the Portuguese; or it is safely stored elsewhere or never existed in the first place.

Conspiracy theories aside, the tooth is almost permanently encased in seven gold caskets within a shrine in the Tooth Temple. Visitors are not allowed into the shrine itself so instead view the tooth's gold caskets from the doorway. The door is opened only twice a day for 30 minutes so tourists only glimpse the relic for a few seconds before the tooth-keepers move the busy line forward.

By all accounts, the temple and the shrine are impressive pieces of either mythology or history with fine architecture and craftsmanship. All things considered I wasn't overly fussed to visit the temple to not glimpse the tooth that probably didn't belong to the Buddha, so didn't bother. I was more interested in the streets, the people and the culture of modern day Kandy.

Kandy is a relaxing and pleasant place to be. Jungle-green hills surround Kandy on every side adding to the city's tranquil and spiritual vibe and the city centre has a liberal scattering of lush plants and trees, particularly along the edge of the lake. I could see the giant white Buddha with his hypothetically offended left knee from all over Kandy, sitting atop his hill keeping a watchful eye out for wicked Gnomes, crooked ministers and the British.

The streets near the central clock tower were clean and nothing like the hectic melee of Galle Road. Here lived upmarket clothes shops, smart restaurants and a wealth of bakeries selling all manner of cheap, tasty bread and pastry treats. There was the usual spicy fish rolls, chicken rolls, beef rolls, vegetable rolls, egg rolls plus the same selection again wrapped in puff pastry instead of a pancake.

Just off the upmarket central area lingered the grubbier, dustier streets filled with gambling joints, liqueur shops, electrical shops, car garages, currency exchanges, more phone shops than any small city needs and a post office that readily accepted my elephant dung birthday card.

Wandering around the streets of Kandy was an enlightening experience. "Hello, which country?" was the usual start from the many smartly-dressed Kandian men who talked to me. "England", I would reply.
"Ah, here for the cricket, yes!?" And then the stranger and I would engage in a friendly chat about cricket, blue whales or other things for a little while. "Do you have a girlfriend?" was usually asked at some tedious point.

One fella shook my hand and said "Ah! Hello! You remember me?"
"Er... no. How do I...?"
"Last night! You bought a chocolate éclair from the restaurant I work."
"Oh, yes! I remember you." We talked about the upcoming cricket match and he recommended a couple of places to eat before we each went about our business.

My business was trying to figure out these Sri Lankans and it's a difficult business indeed. To some extent I was trying to make order from chaos like my attempts to order lunch in The Kandy Muslim Hotel. I ordered a chicken curry and rice and fancied an appetiser. "...and a beef roti, please", I requested.
"Chicken samosa?"
"No, a beef roti."
"Oh, we don't have any beef rotis", he said.
"Ok, a beef samosa."
"Chicken samosa?" he asked.
"No, a beef samosa."
"Fish roll?"
"No, a beef... samosa."

"We don't have any beef, Sir", he informed me.
"No beef?"
"No beef, Sir", he confirmed.
"OK, I'll have a chicken samosa."

When the waiter returned he brought two beef samosas and two fish rolls. The food was delicious and damned-near inedible. Sri Lankans like their food so hot I felt like I was nibbling at the sun. After reading the bill I realised the waiter, probably as confused as I was, had brought a selection of appetisers for me to pick from and only pay for what I took. *Quite clever, really.*

I bought freshly cut mango in the market for a pittance and dawdled round the lake absorbing the city's relaxed, quaint feel. "Bloody hell, what's that?" I blurted aloud to no one in particular. A huge lizard lay basking in the sun on the lakeshore. "That", said a calm gentleman next to me, "is a water monitor; a big, lazy one too." As I continued round the lake I was also treated to a smaller, livelier water monitor, a troupe of monkeys, chipmunks, herons, more wild dogs and loads and loads of fish. From the pavement between the lake and The Temple of the Sacred Tooth Relic I was a little captivated by hundreds of fish writhing over each other racing for the food some kind local teenagers were donating. I stood there, staring.

Behind me, hordes of tourists were busily streaming out of coaches and into the Temple to probably not see the Buddha's old tooth. They went about in their tourist-like fashion completely unaware that the real sight round here was these fish.

Rather close to my ear I heard "which country?" I turned and presenting himself was one plump, middle-aged local chap smiling cordially. "England", I revealed. "Aren't these fish great?" He was a particularly friendly and congenial chap and the usual kind of chat developed. Eventually, he asked if I wanted a ticket to the temple and his cloak of disguise had fallen. He was, of course, a salesman and a particularly good one. As salespeople generally aim to achieve, he was intent on persuading me to do something I didn't really want to do but, growing in resolve, I was determined to resist such persuasion.

"Follow me", he insisted, "this way", but I'd seen this technique before. The guy makes a statement – an instruction disguised as advice. "I'm looking at the fish", I replied. He hid his exasperation in his tone and manner but not his eyes. "Come Sir", he urged with impatience. "Follow me for the temple."

"I want to watch the fish. They're good aren't they?" I invited, but he wasn't interested. Maybe he got bored, frustrated, disheartened or confused but by the time I turned round he had disappeared. *I think I'm learning.*

One young bloke I met wanted to come with me to Dambulla, "for some beers, a good time, see some stuff", he said. *Does he mean as a mate or as a paid guide?* Either way it was too weird.

I sat by the lake outside the Kandian dancing theatre, watching the poor, unsuspecting tourists on their way in, when I met Soma. "Would you like to see the dancing show?" Soma asked me. "Ha, no thanks," I laughed. "I saw it yesterday." Soma added his knowing laugh to mine. I described my tour of Sri Lanka and my quest to see blue whales but, astonishingly, Soma hadn't heard of blue whales. "Huge big things... like fish... in the sea?" It was no use. He just asked and confirmed twice that I didn't have a girlfriend.

Suddenly the rain poured down and Soma took me into a small nearby café and bought me a roti and a samosa. "You should go to Ritigala", he advised. "Ritigala is very nice. Ritigala national park is there. Lots of animals. Not many tourists. They don't go there because they don't know it, but I know it. I can take you there." *I see.* Soma went on to pitch a potential three-day tour around the cultural 'Ancient Cities' region. He dismissed my plan of hopping on a bus to Dambulla as a pointless excursion. "You don't want to stay in Dambulla", he said. "There's nothing there."

It was difficult to know whether or not to trust Soma. I felt sad that previous scamps had made me untrusting of people who might be honest, decent folk. I soon left him and pondered whether this type of meeting was genuine and whether I should expect more of it. One thing was for sure; I was a target and treated as 'different'. *I'm an alien, I'm a legal alien, I'm an Englishman in Sri Lanka,* as Sting didn't quite put it.

Mrs Clement, the dear old lady, had twice accepted my apologies for getting her out of bed at 10:30pm. I sat in her comfortable living room thinking *I should probably eat some fruit* when Mrs Clement presented me with a bowl of delicately prepared fruit.

She had been running her guesthouse since 1982, at first with her husband who had sadly died some time ago. Mrs Clement told a travelling French lady and me stories of previous visitors as she flicked through an old photo album. She had recently been visited by an English lady and her twenty six year old daughter; the mother had stayed with Mrs Clement before the daughter was born and couldn't resist stopping by.

A few houses up the street, she went on, lived the Sangakkara family. She used to see the young boys playing cricket in the street and the smallest boy was always made to field furthest away. His name was Kumar and he went on to make his first appearance for the Sri Lanka national cricket team in 2000. Since then Kumar Sangakkara has been a regular player for Sri Lanka, captaining the side from 2009 to 2011 and winning the ODI cricketer of the year award in 2011. He has made eight double-centuries placing him third in the all-time list of double centuries and is generally regarded as one of the best cricketers in the world.

As I enjoyed my fruit the travelling French lady was trying to find a guesthouse in Negombo, close to Colombo's airport. "I know a nice place you can stay", Mrs Clement helpfully suggested. "The owner is an old lady, like me... but prettier than me," she laughed. *What a sweet old lady.*

Also living with Mrs Clement was her peculiar choice of house helper. Whilst Mrs Clement spoke Sinhalese and English, the helper spoke only Tamil. Sometimes unable to convey her requests, Mrs Clement would just do the tasks herself, hence the early mornings, the early nights and the inconvenience of Englishmen arriving at 10:30pm all the time.

Finally there was Nicky the aggressive Alsatian. This smelly animal filled his day entirely by patrolling the grounds, sleeping and scratching himself. Nicky was endlessly and immediately forgiving to those invited into the house and it quickly became apparent why. The poor blighter was so old he could hardly walk across the room. The prospect of a fight or chase was well beyond him. He impressively convinced as a guard dog, thwarting danger with aggressive barks and knurling teeth but such performances left him staggering back inside the house for long naps.

Pondering the day's events and the people I met I tried to understand how better to get by in Sri Lanka. Everyone was friendly; some wanted a chat, some wanted to sell me something and some wanted to fleece me. I had been lied to by the Taxi drivers at the airport, overcharged on the bus, overcharged in tuk tuks and been accosted by beggars on the beach... I had even been charged considerably more than my Lonely Planet book suggested by dear old Mrs Clement. *This can't go on! I have to figure this out.*

There is no welfare in Sri Lanka - if people don't earn, they don't have, so there are lots of people competing for my business. The more competition, the more fiercely it is competed. It is a game, one that I needed to get better at... and quickly.

In Asia, everything can be negotiated. This is particular true with small businesses be it a tuk tuk driver, a guesthouse, a restaurant, a shop, a guide... virtually anything. They don't have authorisation limits or the reams of policies and procedures dictating prices and what is possible and what isn't. You can put forward a new suggestion for consideration on its own merits. Negotiation is everything here and that evening I set about learning the dark art. The results were thus:-

1. Learn what the standard price should be. Every time I've been overcharged it's because I didn't know what was normal.
2. Tell the other guy that I know what the price should be. If I make sure they know I know what I'm on about they will be less likely to quote outrageous prices.
3. Never accept the first offer. They will always start high – everything is negotiated.
4. Find reasons to lower the price. More people, more nights in a guesthouse, further in a tuk tuk, high competition, no other customers, off-season, any kind of fault with the service, I don't have any more money...
5. Consider the laws of supply and demand. Make it clear I can use someone else.
6. Always agree a price before accepting a service to avoid future antagonism or being overcharged.
7. Let them know that a good price is important to me.
8. Learn a bit of local lingo (hello, thank you) to show respect, friendliness.
9. Treat the other fella as a friend, not an adversary. People are always willing to do a better deal for someone that has treated them with respect and warmth, but don't trust blindly.
10. Act with confidence and clarity. Don't appear a novice. They will take advantage of the naive and uninformed.
11. Be bold. Don't be afraid to negotiate. *Push your luck, son.*

This should stand me in good stead for now. I felt much better and keen to try again. With my rubbish phone I called a guesthouse in Dambulla and confidently negotiated down the price. Then, with one decent deal in the bag, I phoned another guesthouse and negotiated with them, letting them know the price I had already received. It worked like a charm.

One more thing – when I was travelling in Peru we would call everyone 'Amigo'. Because 'Amigo' means 'friend' it starts a conversation off on the right foot. *From here on in everyone will be "my friend".*

At the bus station the next morning a polite, professional and smartly dressed gent kindly pointed me the way to the bus north to Dambulla whilst a less polite, less professional and less smartly dressed gent spat some red stuff onto the floor. *What the hell IS that stuff?*

Chapter 6 – The Cultural Triangle (Part 1)

I wouldn't have the bus driver down as a patient man. With some fifty weary people sat uncomfortably in his bus he charged it up the country to Dambulla like an enraged bull. There was no air-conditioning, only open windows and doors which the conductor repeatedly hung out of touting for fares... but it did have speed. I liked it in part for its urgency and because it had space at the front to stow my backpack, but chiefly because it was 40r (20p).

Dambulla (population 68,200), located in the 'cultural triangle', is made historically significant by the great Dambulla cave temple, ancient caves that have been adopted and elaborately decorated by Buddhist monks over hundreds of years.

Dambulla's day to day focus, though, is industry. The A9 is a major road that travels north from Kandy up the spine of the country to the northernmost city of Jaffna. The A6 is another major road from Colombo travelling north easterly to the northern section of the east coast where it finds Trincomalee. Forty five miles north of Kandy the diagonal A6 meets and merges with the vertical A9 for about 1km before splitting off again to continue its journey to Trincomalee.

Essentially it's a major crossroad but the left and right turns are separated by 1km and clinging to that crossroad like mould on cheese is Dambulla. Its central location, accessibility and throughput of traffic have fuelled its development into a busy, wholesale market town with off-shoot businesses to cater for the masses of visiting workers. Or to put it another way, it's a shit hole. *Blast! Soma was right. I probably should have gone to Ritigala.* My three nights planned here quickly altered to two. *What on Earth am I going to do?*

The first thing I did was flag down a tuk tuk. "The Healey Tourist Inn please, my friend. It's not far", I said to the spritely young driver making sure he knew that I knew where it was crushing any temptations he might have of pulling a fast one. Clever, eh?
"OK, Sir. You staying there, sir?" he asked.
"Yes, two nights I think", I replied.
"I know a nice guesthouse you could stay. It's very nice."
"No thank you. I have a place", I affirmed.
"Oh, it's very nice, Sir. My sister works there. I can take you there."
"No thanks."
"I can get you good price. No problem."

"No thanks", I repeated.

"It's not very far, I..."

"NO!!!" I barked. My startled young driver turned back around sheepishly and didn't say another word. *Oops, a little harsh, perhaps,* I thought, having startled myself, also. It worked though. I checked in with the nice lady in the guesthouse and settled into my room.

I began to feel lonely again. I had enjoyed my time in Kandy and Colombo. It had been interesting, funny, totally new and thought provoking. I had also enjoyed meeting all those people, some more than others admittedly, but none were in a similar position to me, or understood what I was doing. I hadn't been sharing my experiences with anyone so there was no one to talk to, or laugh with, about the events gone by. Even Dammika, as great as he was, wasn't 'in my boat'. *Will it always be like this?* I comforted myself with the knowledge that I'd be at the cricket in a few days, sure to meet some other travelling folk.

Where the blazes is it? I rifled through my backpack and didn't find the book my friend had bought me; a book called 'The man who mistook his wife for a hat' by neurologist Oliver Sacks. *Blast!* After spending time not bending any notes on my harmonica I turned to the other book I'd brought by celebrated physicist, Stephen Hawking.

I had already read Stephen Hawking's 1988 best seller, 'A brief history of time' in which he explained the latest thinking in physics (it goes on about particles, black holes, time travel and the like). In response to feedback that followed (people were less interested in some details but craved expansion on others) he wrote a subsequent book craftily entitled 'A briefer history of time'.

I have the highest regard for Stephen Hawking. Not only is he one of the finest minds physics has ever seen but he has made professional achievements of significant notoriety whilst suffering from the hugely debilitating Motor Neurone Syndrome. He enthusiastically writes in his Foreword, "Today, we are closer than ever to understanding the nature of the universe." *I should hope so, Stephen! It would be a sloppy day's work indeed if we were to end it further away than when we started!*

Early on Hawking gives us the scientific definition of a 'good theory'. A *'good* theory' is one that makes predictions that we can look for in our observations of the world. If our observations are contrary to the theory's predictions then the theory has failed and must be adapted to be consistent with observation again or wiped from existence.

There is a difference of opinion on the definition of a 'theory'. Hawking, physics and science in general take the rigid posture of observable, quantifiable conclusions to be agreed by the academic world. I, meanwhile, hold a more flexible, creative and suggestion-orientated approach where one can authorise its significance oneself. I find that this free-thinking mentality requires much less actual work and, so long as no one bothers to look for ways to disprove it, the glorious possibility of its conclusions remain (if one has been bothered enough to conjure any conclusions).

Granted, I have had less published work than the recognised scientific community (exactly zero) but even so, I am resolved to regard a theory using the definition of my own devising, rather than Science's.

As such my theories have an enviable record of avoiding failure thanks in no small part to resisting the urge to predict anything. Hawking, in response, might well unsympathetically categorise such theories as 'bad theories' whilst I would like to make the subtle, but important, distinction of categorising it as a 'quality-irrelevant theory'. Their contribution to our current understanding of the universe, however, has not yet been thoroughly assessed. We shall revisit Physics later.

The top tourist attraction in Sri Lanka may well be Sigiriya, also known as Lion's Rock (for ease of use for tourists presumably). Sigiriya is a huge, roughly cuboid granite rock which looks to have been plonked in the middle of the flat plains with seemingly no earthly reason to be there. It rises up some 200 metres from its surroundings and its top surface covers roughly 1.5 hectares (perhaps 150 metres by 100 metres). Surrounding the massive rock are gardens and water features that have been built by Kings gone by.

I wondered how this rock came to be and concluded, with healthy amounts of doubt, that the early Earth collided with another celestial body and this huge rock broke off and was hurled through the atmosphere (if there was one) and landed happily in the middle of Sri Lanka. Of course, I have no further observations to support that theory and Stephen Hawking would have no time for it!

We might never know how it got there. During my visit and subsequent research no one seems to offer the slightest speculation as to how a huge granite rock came to be sitting lonesome in the central plains of Sri Lanka. (I did, however, discover the happy fact that Duran Duran filmed their video to their 1982 hit, 'Save a Prayer', here.) That might mean that my theory in the previous paragraph is, pathetically, the foremost theory in current existence, probing further than ever before to explain the existence of Lion's Rock. What a terrible embarrassment to geology that would be.

However Sigiriya came to be, the Sri Lankans have certainly made use of it. In the 3rd century BC, according to Sri Lankan historical documents, it was used as a Buddhist monastery. The trail then went cold until 477AD when begins the famous story of Prince Kasyapa - a tale of deceit, betrayal, revenge and unrestrained stupidity that is told to Sri Lankan children in schools.

King Datusena was a well-loved ruler who made his good name by ambitiously building irrigation tanks and canals for his people. From Anuradapura he ruled the kingdom through more than fifteen years of peace and prosperity.

He had two sons. His first, Prince Kasyapa was born into illegitimacy on the grounds that his Mother was of a lower caste. The second son was Prince Moggallana whose Mother was of Royal standing so he, henceforth, became the rightful heir to the throne.

The prospect of being ruled by his younger half-brother didn't sit well with Kasyapa so he assassinated his father the King by, rather inefficiently, bricking him up in a wall and thus usurped the throne with ease. Moggallana, fearing his own inefficient assassination, fled to India to build an army so he could one day return to claim his rightful place.

Kasyapa was as clever as he was greedy and knew that his brother would return so had the bright idea of building a fortress at the top of the defendable Sigiriya rock. As horny as he was clever, Kasyapa incorporated a pleasure palace into his fortress so he could ease the burden of rule with the comfort of his many, scantily-clad wives.

After many a long and pleasurable year Kasyapa received the fateful news that Moggallana was finally approaching Sigiriya to fulfil his destiny. As such, Kasyapa prepared his forces and led his army from the top of his battle-elephant.

As strategically brilliant as he was horny Kasyapa and his elephant suddenly altered course sidewards to gain a clever strategic advantage but failed to relay this genius insight to his own troops who interpreted the sudden change of direction as a retreat and fled from the battle entirely.

Now alone and defeated Kasyapa drew his knife and with a mighty cry slit his own throat. Moggallana then claimed the throne and moved it back to Anuradapura whilst Sigiriya once more became a Buddhist Monastery.

It is unclear to me what moral-of-the-story Sri Lankan school kids are supposed to pick up from this but I am reliably informed that they are all taught it at school. However, further research has revealed that there are many variations and debate continues about what actually happened. Some accounts cast Kasyapa as the hero and suggest that King Datusena initially suspected Kasyapa was plotting to take the throne and tried to kill him. The King's army attacked Kasyapa but were defeated and King Datusena, with undue haste perhaps, lopped his own head off because he was losing. These accounts go on to say that Kasyapa then became King and built his pleasurable fortress, gardens and water systems in the region during his eighteen year reign. Thus, they claim that the Sri Lankan Department of Education's version does Kasyapa a huge disservice.

Other accounts have Kasyapa down as a randy, sex-crazed 'Playboy King'. They say Sigiriya wasn't a fortress at all but a 'temple of tantric sex initiation' for Kasyapa and his five hundred wives!!

The various stories go into much more depth, introducing many other characters and plots but we've covered the main gist of it here. There's a good chance the actual truth couldn't be found amongst any of it.

I swear the most helpful people in Sri Lanka are in the bus stations. Within seconds of crossing the Dambulla bus station's threshold a multitude of Sri Lankans pointed me to the Sigiriya bus without prompting.

My bus snaked through small villages, picking up local folk and school kids at the many stops on its busy route. *How will I know which stop to get off?* I had thought but my fears, once again, were unfounded as the bus driver shouted to me "You! You get off here!"

"Uhh, pardon", I managed, waking from daydreams.

"Yes, here, get off for you." He'd obviously assumed I was going to Sigiriya. Of course he did. He'd probably never had a white man on his bus that had ever wanted anywhere else.

With Sigiriya standing imposing in the distance I ambled, alone, to find the ticket office and entrance. This was the fifth day of my adventure and my loneliness, though not depressing, was starting to make me feel a little sad. I was not at all embarrassed but would have liked to share the experience with someone, to share ideas, views and jokes.

As I began to climb the rickety metal staircase I heard a gaggle of English voices that came from four young girls someway behind me. Feeling not an ounce of shame I dawdled in the hope they'd catch up with me and I could spark a bit of friendly chat with them.

"I hope you're not afraid of heights", I lamely said when this cunning plan came to fruition.
"Actually, I am", replied one of the four. "I knew this was a bad idea." This was Joanne, a nursing student from Nottingham who, along with two of the others, had come to Sri Lanka to gain some work experience at Kandy's Hospital. "You're doing really well, Jo. Keep going", encouraged Laura.

The fourth girl was Nilli, a delightful Sri Lankan nurse with remarkably good English. For some reason I couldn't decipher she was adamant, vehemently insistant no less, that she wasn't guiding the others round the local sights of interest even though that's exactly what she was doing. They had spent the day being driven around the area with Nilli explaining the relevance of the places they went. Including this disparity the girls were a lot of fun and I instantly felt better.

On the hot, sweaty trudge to the top of the rock the path took us across the face of the wall known as the 'mirror wall'. During the reign of Kasyapa it was decorated with beautiful paintings of buxom women wearing attractive jewellery and little else. I'm not sure why they were topless but I suspect that love-scoundrel King Kasyapa had something to do with it.

Once at the top there were two things to marvel at. Firstly, the surrounding area was so very flat the views were expansive in every direction. It is possible to see various irrigation tanks and canals built so long ago, jungle land, fields of agriculture, local settlements and your half-brother's advancing army from fifty kilometres away.

The other is the fortress ruins on the top of the rock that cover the entire 1.5 hectares of the rock's surface and make for fun exploration. The top of the rock has a few natural rises and falls creating interesting levels within the fortress's construction. Built with thousands of red bricks, there are paths, walls, steps, ledges and water pools. The brick walls rise no higher than the waist; other materials were used that have degraded over the centuries. It would have been interesting to see what it looked like in its full glory in the 5th century.

As I investigated Kasyapa's fortress / pleasure palace my friend Tash's voice appeared in my head saying "that'd be a good place to sneak off with the missus". "Ooh, or there". "And that's a nice, little pool to take a couple of girls". *Tashy and Kasyapa are of like minds,* I decided.

There was a cosy little spot at the far end where some stone steps take the path slightly over the edge of the rock and into a shallow hollow in the rock wall. I could easily imagine a randy Kasyapa taking one or two wives in there for private therapy to help relax from his kingly duties whilst looking out over his stolen kingdom. *This was definitely a pleasure palace*, I decided. I doubt the local archaeologists would accept Tash's testimony but, as far as I was concerned, the mystery was unravelled – the horny little monarch.

At 6pm the girls and I made our descent. By the time we reached the car park it was nearly dark. *Blimey, is it me or does the sun not-half go down quickly round here?*

There was one tuk tuk waiting, primed and ready to charge me a fortune to take me back to Dambulla. Any negotiating attempt on my part was met with 'what else are you going to do?' *Ahh, the economic laws of supply and demand hold considerable sway here. Grrrrr*

"You could come with us in the jeep, Gav", the girls kindly offered. "We've got our own jeep and driver and we're going to Habarana. You can get a bus to Dambulla from there", Nilli informed me. I had no idea where Habarana was but it sounded good to me. I climbed into the back of the open topped jeep and off we trundled.

"You could probably stand up back here", I pondered aloud.
"Actually, we do all the time", said Laura as they all stood up in the back of the jeep and I was delighted to follow suit. It came with only two safety instructions.

1. Duck the overhanging branches;
2. Beware of marauding elephants. *Right you are.*

We sped down the dirt track in the dark, ducking branches and bumping about but no elephants came close, marauding or otherwise. The wind whistled through my hair and, for the first time in days, I shared an exhilarating experience with some friends. It lasted for a fleeting twenty minutes or so and, when they dropped me off as promised at the central crossroads in Habarana, I felt sad at the thought of not seeing them ever again. It was my first contact with other travellers and, though I was only with them for a couple of hours, I missed them immediately.

On the roadside a kind gent volunteered to me that "the bus to Dambulla will be ten minutes". *Everyone knows about the buses in Sri Lanka.* As I strolled to the bus stop I wondered how much credit was left on my new, cheap Sri Lankan phone and, as luck would have it, found a phone stall by the bus stop manned by a couple of young, friendly looking chaps. "Hello my friends", I began, "perhaps you can help. I want to know how much credit I have left". One fella took my phone, dialled in a number which returned a text message displaying my remaining credit. "Wow. What was that number, there?" I asked, and he saved it as a contact in my phone under the name "Acunt". *A bit harsh, fella*, I thought. But still, result!

My bus came promptly and I returned to Dambulla to watch the last 45 minutes of Bangladesh's heroics in nearly winning the Asian Cup final in my local, mosquito riddled bar and reflected on what had turned out to be a marvellous trip to Sigiriya. My pangs of loneliness had been quietened for a short while and I'd had bags more fun thanks to those four girls. A quick look at the map revealed that Habarana is in the exact opposite direction to Dambulla, but it mattered not a jot!

Chapter 7 – The Cultural Triangle (Part 2)

I was up bright and early and as the sun cranked its way up to its usual blisteringly hot form I walked the 1km or so to the Dambulla cave temples talking to myself in an Irish accent. The loneliness was getting to me again so I suppose my mind had felt it necessary to create an Irish friend for me. *If taarking ter meself is der first soign o maadness, Oi don't waarnt ter be sane.* That sentence ashamedly flatters my Irish accent.

My tour began with the four-storey Golden Temple built in the 1970s Birmingham-office-block style with a 30 metre high golden Buddha proudly sat on the roof. This bemusing architectural phenomenon marked the gateway to the Dambulla cave temples. The monastery is found by plodding steadily up the partly-stepped hill riddled with local traders selling water, fresh mango and pineapple, ice creams and carved crafts. Upon arrival one is free to explore the monastery and the five historic temple-caves it boasts.

The earliest evidence of human occupation here is the remains of a skeleton that dates back two thousand seven hundred years. Since then, and with the import of Buddhism, the caves have gradually been developed and decorated with Buddhist paintings and statues.

The largest cave temple is 52 metres long, 23 metres wide and the contributions to its decoration have been plentiful. Upon entering, shoes off if you please, you will find it crammed full with sixteen standing Buddha statues, forty sitting Buddha statues and, just for good measure, statues of the Gods Saman, Vishnu and two kings who made sizable contributions to the monastery's development. The 7-metre high ceiling was covered completely with dozens of identical paintings of Buddha. The five caves hold one hundred and fifty seven statues in total that various Kings have contributed to over the centuries including the impressive 14 metre-long lying Buddha statue carved out of the cave's rock in the 'Cave of the Divine King'.

I couldn't help but feel the mystique, reverence and spirituality of a place adorned in such a way. The smell of burning incense, the earthly glow of light away from the bright sun and the respect of the people in the monastery all add to an atmosphere that imagines an age gone by.

One old, skinny, bearded chap was giving away smiles and coloured threads to tie on the wrist for a small donation. School children, teenagers, groups of young lads and families were all visiting the temple to pay their respects and thanks to Buddha. It felt odd, for some reason, to see the trendily-clad youth of Sri Lanka taking very seriously their tribute to the ancient and spiritual ways. The locals' behaviour in the Dambulla cave temples was a humbling sight to behold and I left in contentment and Irish-sounding contemplation.

Along with Sigiriya and the Dambulla caves temples, the city ruins of Polonnaruwa (population 106,000) fall within an area rich in such history known as the Cultural Triangle. *As I have most of the afternoon left, I might as well hop on a bus and check it out.* Let us begin with the Chola Dynasty.

The Chola Dynasty, at the height of power from the 9th century to the 13th, ruled over most of southern India and became a major power in South East Asia. Having conquered Sri Lanka they moved their Capital from Anuradhapura to Polonnaruwa because it was better defensible and, according to the Lonely Planet Book, to avoid mosquitos. Under their guard it became the first established city in Sri Lanka.

Around the time William the Conqueror was getting to grips with Britain, King Vijayabahu I kicked the Chola Dynasty off the island reuniting the Sinhalese Kingdom once more under a Sri Lankan ruler. He kept Polonnaruwa as his Capital and it remained so for another two centuries.

During this time Parakramabahu took the throne and was determined beyond obsession that not a single drop of rain water shall be wasted. To this end he built advanced irrigation systems that are still used today. The most impressive piece of construction is a vast reservoir called the Parakrama Samudraya (sea of Parakrama) that surrounded the city providing both water and defence. With this Parakramabahu I paved the way for Polonnaruwa to enjoy great success in agriculture and, in turn, trade, giving Polonnaruwa its golden years.

Polonnaruwa's finest hour appears to have now passed. In the 13th century it fell victim to yet more South Indian invaders and the city went into severe decline. To add insult to injury the capital was moved away as was, apparently, the Buddha's tooth which had been residing there – if you'd believe it.

In that golden age statues, monuments, temples, palaces, sanctuaries and gardens were built paying tribute to Polonnaruwa's great successes and devotion to Buddhism. Today, the ruins of these artful constructions are plentiful attracting many visitors each year including, once again, Duran Duran.

I toured the ruins with a podgy, laid-back, middle-aged tuk tuk driver, hired to me by his frustrating and over-intense mate of doubtful sincerity. Despite my unhidden fury, at 4pm he was really the only option. *The laws of supply and demand hold sway. Grrr.*

Most of the ruins are set in a large park with a variety of trees and shrubberies amongst well-kept grassy fields. The podgy man drove me along the quiet narrow roads to each ruin, explained a bit about it on the way and dropped me off pointing to where he'd wait for me.

I encountered an iguana, wild deer, a bunch of pigeons, mischievous looking monkeys and the occasional pod of smartly-dressed school kids saying "hi" or "which country" to me as they stared and smiled.

The least interesting aspect of my tour of the ruins was the ruins. The atmosphere was enjoyably tranquil but didn't stir much wonderment or excitement. Although, there was one mystifying stone dome temple about the size of a theatre but without any discernible way in or out, and I conducted a thorough search. Surely they don't build these huge domes to not allow anyone inside…? The podgy driver was no help. His explanations were sketchy at best as it was. *Perhaps it holds secrets far too valuable to open up for the likes of me.*

At the end of my tour I was returned to the disingenuous miscreant who helped me back to Dambulla by advising me to jump on a moving bus. *What de b-jesus is d-maan getting' me to do dat fer?* Oh, and the podgy man loved his cricket!

By darkness I ambled back toward the guesthouse and stopped off at Dambulla's wholesale market for a nosy. Just off the main road it looked like two huge aircraft hangers with high curved metal roofs sheltering the vast space beneath. The space, however, was packed full with vans, trucks, people and the largest collection of fruit and veg I have ever seen, both in variety and sheer volume. There were lorry loads of produce in huge bags and boxes dumped on the tarmac or waiting patiently on the back of trucks. *Now den, would yer look at dat?*

I saw tomatoes, oranges, apples, cucumbers, onions, cabbages, carrots, pumpkins (???), cauliflowers, water melons, lemons, sweet corn, avocados, dragon fruit, and potatoes, in fact, everything you'd see in the supermarket and a whole bunch of other stuff I didn't recognise. Most of all I saw young Sri Lankan men watching me climb over the mountains of vegetables wondering, *why is some white man with an unforgivable Irish accent wandering around here?* Of course, 'curiosity' is the answer as it is most of the time. Their staring eyes indicated that an intrigued and lost-looking tourist in the market was a break from the normal market humdrum for these fellas and they seemed more-or-less content for me to do what I was doing. For me it was a happy detour on the way back to my less-than-happy guesthouse.

It had been a long and lonely day... again. The Irish accent had kept me company to some extent but there was nothing left to do in Dambulla. I had seen all of the local cultural sights, eaten Kothu, watched cricket in the bar with three locals and a billion mosquitos and even taken a tour of the local wholesale market. And so, because I was making this journey through time and space, I thought I would spend the rest of the evening learning about time and space with Stephen Hawking.

It is easy as a child to be left amazed at the encyclopaedic amount we know about the Universe and wonder at how we humans have found things out. As an adult it is easy to be left amazed at the infinitely vast amount we don't know about the Universe.

Children just don't know what they don't know whereas adults sometimes do know what they don't know. You are at a disadvantage if you don't know how to know what you don't know compared with someone who does know how to know what they don't know. Similarly, it is important for someone to know how to know what he does know, if only to help him figure out how to know what he doesn't know.

Billions of pounds, euros or dollars have been spent on the much-acclaimed Large Hadron Collider in Geneva committed on the agreed knowledge that we didn't know something. We knew that we didn't know if the Higgs Boson particle existed and were so certain of not knowing it that all of this economic wealth was, and still is, being invested in the project.

There might be many other particles out there we don't know about. If only we knew which ones we don't know about we could invest billions more into learning about them.

Stephen Hawking knows a lot and he says he hardly knows anything at all. He does, however, know about a chap called Friedmann and explains at some length about Friedmann's three different kinds of model for the universe of which one must be reality... pretty much. These were;

1. a slowly expanding universe which gravity will eventually stop and start shrinking it again,
2. a quickly expanding universe which gravity will never stop, but might slow down a bit,
3. a carefully balanced, slightly expanding universe where the rate of expansion will gradually slow down over time but never quite stop.

Friedmann includes all sorts of details about how each model could come to be, and how the universe behaves in each scenario, but which is the correct model? The answer, Hawking goes on to explain, was found using Edwin Hubble's red-shift technique of measuring a star's speed away from us. He found that other stars and galaxies are not only moving away from each other, they are **accelerating** away from each other. But the attractive force of gravity should, as far as we thought, be pulling everything together.

After all that, the chapter concludes that the Universe is, in fact, expanding at an ever-increasing rate and none of Friedmann's models apply, and we still don't know why. *Thanks Stephen.*

All of this work has not been in vain, however. We now know that we know the Universe is expanding at an increasing rate and we know that we don't know why the hell that is, though we suspect it has something to do with dark matter (which we know very little about) or dark energy (which we know even less about). We also know that Friedmann didn't know what he thought he knew, and we know that Hawking knows Friedmann didn't know what he thought he knew. Hawking also knows everything we know and, no doubt, considerably more. In fact, Professor Hawking probably knows more of what he doesn't know than what we know we don't know… and he knows it!

An extra bonus to this cosmological saga is a theory that suggests that the galaxies are not travelling further away from us more quickly at all. Instead, on the edge of space where the oldest parts of the universe are, it is time that is expanding and that has affected our measurements. In essence, a second is a bit shorter than it used to be. Government cuts and all that, I suppose.

Goodnight, then!
Aye! And a goodnight ter you, den dere, feller.

Chapter 8 – Induruwa

The cricket was to start in two days in the south coast city of Galle and, wandering around Dambulla bus station, I was as far north as I was going to go. Some splendid people pointed me to the right bus and spat red stuff on the floor.

To travel over half the length of the country by bus took nearly the whole day and cost me an entire £2.50. I changed buses in Colombo for Induruwa, a beach town just an hour north from Galle that is so small it's almost not there. The journey was sprinkled with local peddlers climbing aboard to sell flattened and skewered barbequed chickens, vegetable rolls and various other snacks wrapped in children's homework.

To help pass the time I thought to myself in an Australian accent and pondered the traffic rules of the inter-city highways which appeared to differ greatly to those I observed in Colombo. The fruits of my labour culminated in the following.

The Gods of the roads are the buses – and it's Old Testament stuff. They are the pinnacle of the food chain, bullies of the road and Lords and Masters of all they survey. Such is the buses' dominance they sometimes commandeer the right of way on the wrong side of the road to overtake some mere mortal vehicle, inclining oncoming traffic to pull onto the grass verge.

Time waits for no man and neither do Sri Lankan bus drivers. He who rides the bus can rest assured that the driver is fully committed to getting them there immediately. The driver's daring and impatience knows no bounds, regularly achieving overtakings unseen in England. Also, the bus will do anything to avoid stopping. To pick people up they reluctantly slow down just enough for people to jump on or off. But generally the accelerator pedal is pressed solidly to the floor else the brake pedal is. Every risk and short-cut is seized upon to considerately shave a few seconds off everyone's journey time.

Every vehicle chooses one noise for its horn and that noise remains the same regardless of the driver's message. My old much-loved Renault 19's horn used to sound "toot toot", which is to say "Ahem... pardon me, I'd like to squeeze through if I may." The Sri Lankan buses' horn is used minutely and has the sound of several furious bulls only more aggressive, and without care for courtesy shouts "GET OUT OF MY WAY, YOU MAGGOTS!!!!" If the Sri Lankan bus driver hits his horn to say

"Hello, just letting you know I'm here", or "Ayup Barry, it's me, Bernard", the listener will actually hear "GET OUT OF MY WAY, YOU MAGGOTS!!!!"

The buses may be old and uncomfortable but they provide a fast, cheap and regular service for the country's people, and it is pleasing to see that a bus full of some forty uncomfortable travellers take precedence over other road users. I thought they were splendid.

During the journey I also pondered the tuk tuk drivers. There are so many of them competition is extreme and so, in order to get ahead, they learn a few tips from Satan about marketing.

You might as well know now, or perhaps you know already, that the concept of Marketing originated in the bowels of hell. As a trusting naïve young child I assumed the good people in the companies of our free market to be honest, upstanding citizens and any wrong doers would be rooted out and shot... or at least blackballed, fired and jailed. Maybe they were at one time, but I have since discovered that Marketing Departments are nests of devious liars trying convince the world, including themselves, that they're not liars.

Their finest achievement is to market themselves as 'Marketing' instead of the collection of modern-day tricksters they are. They will tell you "everything we say is perfectly true" and if you look at what they've said at face value they'll usually be right. But communication is to transfer an idea, a meaning or an image and words / numbers / graphics are only tools to help us do that. Although their carefully constructed sentences and statistics are true at face value they convey a false meaning, impression or image and it's entirely deliberate. They manipulate the inherent pieces of inefficiency of communication. "We've only got two left, Sir", they might say, implying that lots of people have bought this product when actually they only had two in the first place. "This is now half price, Sir, a real bargain", when they doubled the price to start with. They'll tell the world the good bits but won't mention the bad bits. "This laptop has the fastest processor in its price range, Sir", but it only lasts 3 months. Or they can release some subjective, opinionated stuff like "this is great, amazing. I love it", that is so vague it can't technically be disproved. They may even present a satisfied customer saying "I was given a fantastic service and was really pleased", but they never present the poor sod who said "they fucked me right over! What a complete bunch of bastards!" It wouldn't do any good for sales, of course, but in communicating to the world what their service is like they present a one-sided image.

The most frustrating thing about marketing is that... well... we need it. We need companies to tell us what their product is and what it can do for us, but one day, one utter bastard manipulated his message to get himself ahead and everyone else would continue to lose business until they did the same.

This 'getting ahead' happens everywhere and in the end no one is relatively better off. Imagine, if you would, an ambitious and talentless fella who one day thought to get ahead by being the first bloke to iron his shirt. By looking smarter he held an advantage over the other chaps who were eventually resigned to ironing their shirts too. Now the jolly lot of them spend half an hour on a Sunday ironing their shirts for no extra gain whatsoever apart from the owner of the iron shop who has since bought a villa in Greece.

And so, I surmise, it goes with tuk tuk drivers. With competition this intense one fella once thought to win some fares by, for instance, telling tourists that there are no buses and all the others had to invent their own sneaky tactics to keep up. Now, the common tuk tuk driver has developed an array of sales, marketing and negotiation tactics to win business. It's not their fault; they have to because that first greedy git started the whole merry-go-round in the first place.

I must stress here that striving to get ahead in a respectful and proper manner gives the world new innovations, improved products, gives people the chance to pursue their dreams and rewards the ones who work to make things better. I'm just merely pointing out that it can sometimes drive people to use unsavoury methods... and that Marketing is the devil's work!

Eventually I arrived at the charming Long Beach guesthouse in Induruwa and welcomed by a tall, kind French lady and her smaller and balder Sri Lankan husband. Their spacious back porch looked over a pleasant garden and the beach beyond. I was hot, sweaty and sticky and desperately looked forward to that first dive in the Indian Ocean.

That first dip in the sea always comes with a little apprehension. The cold sea is stark in its refreshment and, at the age of 33, I had learned to be ready for it. I had never needed to not prepare myself so much - the sea was as warm as a bath. *How queer.* Apparently it doesn't vary by more than a few degrees all year.

I rinsed off the dried, sticky sweat my skin had acquired on the long bus journey and lolloped about the Indian Ocean by this beautiful beach, palm trees and a sun filled blue sky. I'm not a beach man by any means but this was just fine, even though the current was trying to drag me back up the coast to Colombo.

At dinner, sat on the porch, were Copper Steve and Dave, two middle-aged Englishmen who were kind enough to support their cricket team in Sri Lanka and invite me to join them for dinner. I was pleased of the company, and good company it was too. I explained that I had come to Sri Lanka to see the blue whales and that I'd try to meet with Asha de Vos. Copper Steve laughed and scoffed away any chance of that. He was by far the more talkative of the two and told me a few particularly interesting experiences and stories that his job had given him.

Steve spends a lot of time working football matches trying to make sure hooligans don't destroy the towns or the people in them. It is a bizarre thing that football hooligans arrange to fight each other. I can't understand it. Try as I might I don't have a theory that explains hooliganism and organised fights but I would like to listen in on the phone conversation...

"Alright, mate. It's Nasty Carl from Millwall. Is that Big Joe?"
"Yeah, alright Nasty, how's it going? I heard you lot got smashed up in Stoke last month. They're in pretty good form aren't they?"
"Hell of a rumble, that one Joe. They've got a couple of new lads who are pretty handy. One of them broke our Terry's arm!"
"Bloody Hell, I bet your Terry's pissed off about that. He must be ready to tear their heads off next year, ha ha ha. Anyway, you must be calling about next Saturday - fancy a fight? Is there a bunch of you coming down to Shrewsbury?"
"Yeah, it's Smilin' Brian's birthday so we thought we'd make a weekend of it. Have a few pints, something to eat, watch the second half of the game, maybe, and have a punch up behind the train station like last year. Brian loved last year. He got a brick in the face, broke his nose, picked up the same brick and broke your guy's nose. He's always going on about that. So are you up for it?"
"Sure, it's always a good fight with you lot, but tell that fella of yours with a tattoo of his girlfriend's tits on his face not to hit people with a motorbike chain. Our Charlie's still pissed off that his new Tommy Hilfiger shirt got ripped. Only knuckle dusters, wooden batons and steel toecaps, Ok? You know what I'm like about fair play."
"No worries, Big Joe. Will you be able to get rid of the rozzers?"

"Yeah, we'll pay some kids to chuck bricks through the Red Lion windows on the other side of town. Get the coppers over there."
"Nice one, Big Joe. Sorted. See you then, and give my love to the wife."

According to Copper Steve, one of the meanest hooligan rivalries in Britain is between the two big Welsh clubs, Cardiff and Swansea. They hate each other bitterly. If Cardiff City are playing a long way away their hooligans might just pop over to Swansea and fight them instead. They could be home in time for tea. It's a rivalry steeped in a history and tradition of deep-set hatred.

Loyalties get a bit confused, however, when Wales play. The Welsh hooligans are, understandably, made up primarily of Cardiff hooligans and Swansea hooligans. It has been known for them to travel across Europe with Wales and start fighting each other. Quite what the home hooligans think when they see that I can't imagine. *Zis Vales iz crazy!*

Copper Steve relayed a story from a colleague about Wales' trip to Azerbaijan. Most Wales supporters stayed in a large central hotel where one large Azerbaijan bloke wearing urban army combats marched into the lobby and shouted "VALES!!! HOW MANY MEN DO YOU 'AVE!!?"
….silence….

"VAAALES!!!!! HOW MANY MEN DO YOU 'AVE!!!!?"
Eventually, a prominent Cardiff City hooligan called back, "ERR… ABOUT FIFTY!"
The challenger immediately responded, "FIFTY OF YOU, FIFTY OF US!! IN ZEE SQUARE, VON HOUR!" and off he marched.

It's a crazy world for sure. Copper Steve doubted that Azerbaijan would restrict their numbers to fifty. No one wants to be sat on the bench, I suppose.

Copper Steve's stories were enjoyed over a nice mug of beer. Our guesthouse owner, a shrewd and clever individual who charged a 15% service charge on everything without discrimination, was making full use of the alcohol license he didn't have.

In Sri Lanka it is very difficult to obtain a license to sell alcohol. Rumour has it the big players bribe certain people to be granted one and with the only license in town they charge a high price for the beer.

Our guesthouse owner told us about a man who refused to pay the bribe for his alcohol license. The powerful councillors sent round some rude and damaging blokes to 'have a word' with him and his shop.

He bravely took his story to the newspapers and managed to get his way, surprisingly surviving the whole ordeal.

Given the scarcity of alcohol licenses and that beer was not being sold by less shrewd local businessmen our guesthouse owner charged a healthy price for his beer and served it in coffee mugs. Officially, of course, he didn't serve us beer at all. Not only did he charge us a high price for beer he can't sell us he charged his 15% service charge for serving beer he can't serve us! I told you he was clever. And he loved his cricket.

Before Steve and Dave retired to bed they invited me to join them in a taxi to Galle the following day. I said that maybe I would - the beauty of travelling like this is that you can go with the flow. Should I meet a couple of attractive and pleasant German girls I can hang around with them for a while instead.

I remained on the porch to read some Stephen Hawking and met a couple of attractive and pleasant German girls. Astrid and Maggie were nearing the end of their three week backpacking holiday. Maggie spoke excellent English, was cute, chatty and funny. Astrid was shyer and less confident with her English but lovely and personable. They stopped for a chat and a joke about our cunning guesthouse owner. "How much of a service is it to fetch a bottle of water?" *Well, quite right, Maggie.* We arranged to meet for breakfast and visit a turtle sanctuary just down the road.

My loneliness from the previous few days began to dissipate thanks to an enjoyable evening with Steve and Dave, the German girls and a chat about cricket with our friendly, money-grabbing guesthouse owner. I hoped this would be the start of meeting a few more people.

The following day Maggie and Astrid told me about the hassle they had received from 'beach boys'. Sri Lankan people believe quite strongly in no-sex-before-marriage and the young lads hanging around the beach have gathered that western girls, on the whole, don't. That nugget of information acts like Viagra to these boys and they pursue any white girls they find scantily-clad on the beach. Maggie and Astrid, however, were German and took no nonsense from any happy-go-lucky chancers.

I witnessed some of this 'beach boy' behaviour first-hand at the turtle sanctuary. Our personal guide was a young, confident, overweight and dislikeable lad who had met my two new German friends on the beach the previous day and tried to lure them to his party. He explained briefly and unenthusiastically about the turtles, preferring instead to entice Astrid and Maggie to his family's restaurant with the best table and a party afterwards. He was all smiles and bravado, quips and jests with the girls and gave them a medium sized, blind turtle to cuddle, but made no acknowledgement of my presence whatsoever.

Despite my keen observations, needle sharp wit and insightful questions the most I could extract from his flapping, over-used mouth was "Uh". When I spoke he looked at me with narrowing eyes that said "Fuck off, pal. I wish you were dead. Me and these white girls are having a party and your worthless existence is spoiling it."

"Your water pools are very small for these poor turtles. Isn't that very mean?" I commented.

"Yes... they hate it, look", agreed Maggie, looking at our generously-fed guide. "Can't you make things nicer for them?" *Ha, wriggle out of that, fatso.*

The sanctuary itself summoned mixed emotions. They successfully boost the turtle population by securing and protecting vulnerable turtle eggs found on the beach. The eggs hatch in the sanctuary and, eventually, dozens of baby turtles are released into the sea saving them from the hazards of predators, poachers and mis-navigation by trying to get to the sea all by themselves.

The sanctuary also houses adult turtles who, for one reason or another, wouldn't be able to survive in the wild. Some were blind, some were mutilated and one little fella was albino. "He is bright colour, so sharks can see him easily", we were told.

As noble a cause as that may seem they were kept in miserable conditions. Typically six turtles reside in a grey, concrete 2 metre-square tank without vegetation or anything of any interest. They were washed and given pieces of fish from time to time, and that is their life. If I was a 3-legged turtle I'd rather take my chances in the wild than stay there. *Worse things don't always happen at sea.* Whilst scuba diving in Thailand in 2007 I met a wild 3-legged turtle unkindly known by the locals as 'Stumpy' and he seemed alright...

We hung out on Induruwa's beautiful beach for a while. Astrid and Maggie were eager to grab a tan to take back to Germany and I went to explore a big, black, craggy rock that stuck out of the beach and stretched into the sea. I climbed the near side of it and spotted a little black crab scuttle sidewards over the top ridge. Slowly, I climbed and peered over the ridge but the crab had disappeared. With one more step the whole side of the rock moved as dozens of black crabs scuttled sideward, startled by my curiosity. *Ha, found you.* The sneaky little critters had been hiding behind their own camouflage and my unsatisfactory human eyesight. As I stood there watching them scamper about I could almost hear them laugh as a mighty wave crashed against the rock and drenched me from top to toe. *Blast!*

    Wet through I said my warm goodbyes to Maggie and Astrid and paid virtually nothing for a thrilling bus-ride to Galle.

Chapter 9 – First Day in Galle

Galle (population 90,270) is the fourth largest city in Sri Lanka and lies on the south west corner of the teardrop island. One of its two main attractions is the fort, an old-town area that fills a peninsular roughly 500 metres wide that juts a kilometre out to sea. A 20 metres high stone wall surrounds the fort area, looming over the sea on three sides and the land-entrance on the fourth.

Once upon a time Galle was the major port city of Sri Lanka and held a prominent position for sea-trade routes. As such, the Portuguese took Galle for themselves by force in the 16th Century and, clearly thinking the cit defences were a breeze to overwhelm, promptly built a fort. In 1663 the Dutch arrived, gained occupancy of Galle and unceremoniously demolished the Portuguese's attempt at a fort and built a new one. They had done a far better job of it according to the British who, upon their occupancy from 1796, retained the Dutch fort and thus it remains today.

The Dutch and the British were proven sound judges on matters of fortification when the fort walls held firm to protect most of the old town from the ferocious tsunami of 2004 that devastated so much of Asia.

The other main attraction in Galle is the Galle International Stadium and the cricket that is played there. It sits directly outside the fort exactly where the peninsula joins the mainland and the imposing fort wall stands guard at one end casting its charm over the ground. This ground is known to be one of the most picturesque International cricket grounds in the world and for good reason. From the photographs alone I knew I had to come here.

Now then, good reader, you may be a lover of cricket or you may not. I have known it be said that cricket is "boring". After having it explained to me that I couldn't have those people shot I was made to realise that some people may never have had the chance to commit the time to understand the game.

If this is you, fear not. I see now it's not your fault. If only circumstances had been different you too could have invested your time in test cricket and become worldly wise with it. Obviously mistakes have occurred and the system has failed you. Don't worry, there is still time.

It took me a few years during my twenties to understand enough the many facets of the great game to fully appreciate it.

Essentially, the bowler makes the ball pitch in front of the batsman in a way that will create some unpredictable movement or deviation so that the batsman will make an error and, as the bowler hopes, get out. That simple situation creates any number of considerations including the condition of the ground where the ball pitches, the condition of the ball, the strengths, weaknesses and form of the bowlers and batters, the weather, the field positions, players' mental states and much else that can affect the strategy a team chooses to adopt. There is so much to talk about that the TV and radio commentators seem to have no trouble talking all day for the full five days of a Test. Even when whole days of cricket are wiped out for unfavourable weather reasons the commentators continue to vivaciously discuss the endless and fascinating angles of the game that isn't currently occurring. It's almost as if they are grateful to be able to properly discuss the cricket without being interrupted by the actual cricket.

The game in Galle was a five day Test where each team bats twice, but if they run out of time the game is declared a draw. Tests didn't used to last 5 days; they used to be 'timeless' and carried on until both teams had completed both of their innings, but this eventually created logistical and commercial complications.

The last timeless test was in March 1939 when England played South Africa in Durban. By the tenth day of play England were batting the fourth innings chasing a target of 696 to win and managed an incredible 654 for 5 before the game was abandoned for a draw because the England players had to catch their boat home.

The Galle Test is the first of a two-Test series; the second in Colombo starts ten days later. Most cricket-supporting Englishmen in Galle had wisely booked their accommodation in advance (including me at some £25 a night for six nights) fearing accommodation to be impossible to find on arrival given the hordes of English cricket fans descending onto Galle - and descend they did. It was reported that some 15,000 English fans had come to Galle, twice as many as had been predicted and nearly 17% of Galle's population. I had booked a room inside the fort area at 'The Admiral's House'. *I wonder what the Admiral is like...*

My bus arrived into Galle around 7pm and I was looking forward to finding the Admiral and his house, having an extravagant meal and getting my bearings. The Galle bus station was conveniently located by the cricket ground and fort area and my bus inconveniently dashed straight past it and charged another mile up the road before letting me off. *Bugger!!*

Annoyed, I began the mile-long trudge back towards the fort in the dark fully laden with backpack and day-rucksack. The shadowy streets were eerily quiet with only the occasional stray dog or shadowy fella occasionally spitting some red stuff on the floor. The place was grubby, littered and shabby but the excitement of the cricket wouldn't allow my spirits to drop. The Indian Ocean lapped the shore to my left as I passed shops, eateries and banks.

BANKS! Great! For some unknown reasons less developed countries all suffer from a catastrophic dearth of small change so it's important always to carry a bunch of small notes. This quickly becomes one of the major considerations of travelling. With that in mind I thought of a neat trick. If you want 5,000r from a cash machine don't ask it for 5,000r otherwise you'll get five, 1,000r notes. Instead, request 4,900r so that it reluctantly gives you some small notes too.

After an hour's more plodding, searching and enquiring I found The Admiral's House and his friendly, limping butler gave me a warm welcome. He spoke English only slightly but that didn't impede his enthusiasm for a friendly chat one bit and I could barely understand anything he said. Mostly I gleaned that he was shocked I was here on my own.

The first day of the Test and I awoke to the beautiful, exotic song of a bird outside my window, a tropical cock-le-doodle-do no less, and a cup of extra sweet Sri Lankan tea given to me by the Admiral's butler who courageously took the opportunity to ask me if I had a girlfriend.

Galle had woken to find itself, once again, occupied by the English. I arrived at the ticket office just in time for a cataclysmic disaster; the first two days of the cricket had sold out. What's more the ticket pricing at 5,000r (£25) for English fans and 200r (£1) for local fans had started the wagings of war.

There was uproar from the English newspapers and the fans on tour alike and knowing that the Sri Lankan Cricket Board charged Australian fans only 200r when they came here did little to quell the tempers. Neither did the rumour that the Sri Lankan Cricket Board was broke and was using our visit to refill their coffers and perhaps pay their players for the first time in months.

There was much discussion amongst the fans as to the rights and wrongs of it. Some hated that they would treat the locals and tourists differently, some didn't mind being treated differently but thought the disparity was excessive whilst others had the Sri Lankan Cricket Board down as a bunch of crooks who charged whatever they thought they could get away with. It did no good for Anglo-Sri Lankan relations whichever way you sliced it.

In the end the English fans who bought a ticket for £25 were furious. The English fans who couldn't buy a ticket for £25 were furious and the English fans who never tried to buy a ticket sat on top of the fort wall in splendid singing voice and contented jubilation.

With freshly absconded enthusiasm I sauntered my way towards the fort wall by skirting round the ground. "Hssssssss", I heard from beneath my feet and looked down. "AAAAARRGGHH!!!" A huge, spikey and seriously miffed water monitor poked his head and teeth out of the drains. *Bloody hell, there are water monitors in the drains!* This unfortunate frightening reptile had woken up to swarms of Englishmen stomping all over his territory.

The drains in Galle consist of a concrete trench a bit over a foot deep and wide that runs by the side of the pavement covered with paving slabs. The odd slab was missing and this water monitor looked at me through the gap thinking *nobody told me the cricket was on today* before retreating deeper into his drains to sulk away from the barmy bloody world outside.

And indeed it was barmy, the Barmy Army to be precise - that water monitor couldn't have been more right. Non-cricketers may not be aware of the Barmy Army, but the entire cricketing world is. The Barmy Army originally started as a small group of fans who followed English cricket all over the world creating a carnival atmosphere wherever they went. It has now evolved into a large organisation and business, providing coordinated cricket holidays, a magazine, newsletters and access to England tickets. They have become so iconic that people often say "Barmy Army" when they just mean "England fans". On top of all that they have a trumpeter who fills the ears and hearts of the English supporters with pride and joy virtually every time England play cricket.

I was still skirting the ground when I happened upon an unguarded open gate. There was lots of English fans on the other side so

I popped my head through and clapped eyes on a topless, tattooed, Londoner tying his flag to the fence. "Excuse me", I said "am I OK to come in here?" to which he gave a wicked smile and replied, "Yer in aren't, ya?" *Well, I suppose you're quite right, squire.* And so I glided through just as, it turns out, every other early-riser in there had.

I found out later that this was the local's enclosure, although there were no locals in there, nor shade nor seating for that matter, but we had a grassy bank and a view from directly behind the fort end. We were all glad to be there, especially when we saw there was a bar selling half a pint of beer at the reasonable price of 150r (75p). Despite the sold out tickets and its related war, and that disgruntled water monitor, things were picking up.

It was 9:30am and already very hot. One must take a hat, water and sun cream if one wants to enjoy a full day's play in Sri Lanka. It would also help to have some money for food unless you happen to be canny Yorkshire folk like Mick and Karen.

In their fifties, this enormously friendly couple were Yorkshire through and through, other than the fact that they were from Derbyshire. A 'new' Yorkshire man might say "aye" instead of "yes" but an old-school Yorkshire man will say "ah". I know this because I had some Yorkshire speak lessons from an old-school Sheffielder who was fluent in old Sheffield, new Sheffield and Barnsley. His native language was old Sheffield ("ah"), spoken with the family but he would respectfully use new Sheffield ("aye") when at work.

Mick and Karen, quite remarkably, had left their beloved Yorkshire behind three and a half years previous and had been travelling around Asia ever since. Between the rent for their house and a pension they gather £140 a week and can afford to travel round Asia endlessly. They go where they want, when they want, see what they want to see and get over to Sri Lanka to watch the cricket. In that time they have been back to England once to see their daughter's graduation and have had one family Christmas in Australia! They love it. They had spent the previous four months in Cambodia - I will be lucky to have three weeks there.

As soon as I mentioned to Mick and Karen that I was from Sheffield I was warmly embraced into the family. "Tha can tell a Yorkshireman, but tha can't tell him much". The talkative Mick and I spoke about cricket at length. If the umpires made an erroneous decision, "a Yorkshire man wouldn't have done that", was Mick's condemnation. If the prices were too high "a Yorkshire man wouldn't pay that." What a Yorkshire man would do, it seems, is sneak through an open gate at the cricket and bring his own food which Mick and Karen kindly shared with me.

This is why cricket is so good. I'll admit it requires a bit of patience sometimes but one can just sit back, have a beer and a chat, talk cricket, see the story unfold throughout the day and be lifted by the occasional burst of excitement or exhibit of flair whilst making new friends. What could be more pleasant?

As the morning grew older the sun grew stronger and it was getting too much for some on our grassy bank. Two gents stumbled along half carrying an old, portly English fellow and asked if we could make room for him to sit down because he's not feeling well. His smart white beard matched his smart white hair. He wore a Sri Lankan cricket t-shirt, cream chino trousers and a cream sun hat. As he plonked his lardy arse on the grass I knew the man was cricket through and through... and that he'd probably had an early snifter of sherry.

I offered him some water and asked if he was feeling OK, to which he replied in a rather posh accent, "I don't think I should have come on this trip. It's my legs you see, they're knackered."
"Ah" said Mick.
"63 years", he continued, "63 years I've been playing cricket. It takes its toll you know. I had to give it up last year. Started when I was 16."
Blimey, this fella is 80!
"Were you a bowler or a batter?" I asked.
"Oh, a batsmen... for the first 50 years at least. Then I started to bowl a few nice, gentle overs when the legs started to go."
"Ah... ah" said Mick.

I'm sure the rest of his team were delighted with his gentle dibbly-dobblers though they seem befitting of this gentle chap. I left him in peace to watch the cricket and he used the time to topple sideward and vomit on his trousers. *Those old, knackered legs of his I suppose.* Shortly after that his two kind helpers carried him off to one of the air-conditioned seating areas further round the ground. I checked on him later and he seemed much more comfortable.

I had to admire his gusto to get out here for the cricket. It's pleasing to see that the man's sense of adventure hadn't diminished with age. Driven with the natural English urge to watch cricket he had travelled half way round the world, creaking body and all, to cope with whatever happens when it happens. Maybe he was coping or maybe he wasn't but one can't deny he *was* in Sri Lanka watching the cricket.

And so we idly blazoned our way through the day. Sri Lanka's runs began to flow, so did the sun cream and so did the beers. I got myself in a round with three pleasant lads next to me, Tom, Will and Lawrence who I can tell you nothing more about but my involvement in the round made the beer drinking a shave more efficient. The sun became intense but, by focusing on the cricket, the friendly chat and the occasional sing song, I could keep my mind off it.

Once the cricket stopped for lunch or tea I walked half way round the ground to bask in some shade. A small game of cricket sprung up in front of the stands. Some loutish looking English lads were having a mock game with a tennis ball and a small bat and encouraged the hovering Sri Lankan school kids to have a bat or a bowl at every opportunity. One young lad demonstrated some devilish spin and, much to his pride and joy, saw his bowling beamed onto the big screen and around the world courtesy of the Sky broadcasters. *It's the stuff dreams are made of.*

Cricket has none of the hooliganism that Copper Steve regaled. It is so very friendly and gentlemanly. I love the expression "son, always play with a straight bat". On the one hand that is sound batting instruction, especially when the bowlers are finding variable bounce, but it is also wisely advising honesty to others and to oneself.

##Beep beep##. I received a text message on my Sri Lankan rubbish phone. *Who the hell would be texting me on this number?* It turned out that Kish, the friend I had made in that joyless Department of Immigration, was also in the ground and wanted to gloat about his free food, drink, and air-conditioning from the comfort of the VIP lounge. He kindly invited me to have evening dinner at his family home. *How marvellous.*

2:45pm and Tea. The Sri Lankan batsmen had seen off the worst of the English bowling attack, we supporters had seen off the very worst of the sun and the atmosphere on our grassy bank was about to explode. It turned out that, at tea, the gates open to allow cricket fans into the ground for free to see the last two-hour session of the day.

Sri Lankans poured into our enclosure to watch their captain, Mahela Jayawardene, smash the England bowlers around the ground and they loved it. A group of young, exuberant Sri Lankan men stood close to us singing their hearts out with broad smiles on their faces. Chants of "Sri Lanka Army!!! Sri Lanka Army!!!" rang out before, with uncommon generosity, they sang "Barmy Army!!! Barmy Army!!!" The hearty mix of drunken cricket fans and colourful characters created plenty of healthy fun and banter, all overjoyed at watching our teams in an International Test. One particularly charitable fellow told me "You can kiss my girlfriend… because I love you!" *What a friendly fella.* His girlfriend wasn't there, mind you. Still, in all the sporting events I've been to I've never seen such gracious hospitality. You don't get that at Port Vale!

Chapter 10 – Galle (Part 1)

Kish's hospitality came with but one request. "Gavin, can I please ask that you don't get drunk", he said when his mother left us each with a glass of Old Arrack and lemonade. Maybe he didn't want me to show him up or perhaps he regarded his two drunken uncles as all the drunks the house could take. Either way the fact that he asked was a huge victory in my mind because I had already been striving to hide the fact that I'd been drinking all day.

Kish and his family lived in a beautiful, large house and Kish's Father was preciously proud of his pristine garden. He gave me the grand tour showing me his prosperous coconut trees, fruit trees, exotic flowers and crisp lawn. He'd put much love into it, I could see; it's a shame Kish wants to build another house over it. Obviously, Kish's Father asked me if I had a girlfriend.

The love Kish's Dad had put into his garden was matched by the love Kish's Mum had put into our dinner. I couldn't believe it when I learned it was just for Kish and me. She had prepared a delicious feast for at least six people with rice, three curried dishes, devilled chicken, chicken wings, cucumber and tomato salad, egg salad, dhal and for dessert, ice cream and grapes. Most of that was as wildly hot as every other Sri Lankan meal and I carefully nibbled at each lest burn holes in my cheeks. We ate until we were stuffed and made only a dent. *Well done, Mrs Kish.*

Having witnessed the fun of the Barmy Army Kish had decided to trade being cool, fed and watered alone in the corporate box for the carnival atmosphere of the stands. Willing to take whatever the sun could throw at us in exchange we planned to meet early in the morning and glide through that gate.

Before I left the two drunken uncles gave me enormous friendly hugs and insisted on a group photograph. They made me feel like we were best mates.

Ever the pacifist I stayed out of the ticket wars. I watched all of the cricket and didn't buy a ticket for any of it. When I met up with Kish in the morning the security had picked up some form and had the gate well-guarded. With all tickets sold out we moved swiftly on to plan B – corruption!

I have previously done some experiments with bribery. My friends Tash, Marcus and I went to Staffordshire's V-Festival in 2008 in Tashy's campervan. On the drive there we realised that we had erroneously failed to buy a campervan field ticket and so, in the hours available to us, devised a meticulously calculated and considered plan to bribe the fella on the gate. He'd be working the festival because he hadn't got much money and £30 or £40 would stretch a long way for his weekend.

Having not undertaken such skulduggery before we were very nervous. In the half hour between polishing the finer points of the plan and our arrival we nurtured the dark mental forces required for bribery in our psyche, fighting against years of playing with straight bats to appear like credible and authentic bribers come the moment. Amongst the angst there was also mild curiosity about how this bribe was going to unfold. Would he go for it? Would he laugh in our faces… report us?

When the moment came we chose our bribery target who said, "No ticket? No problem, you can buy a ticket here", and so we did. So that was that, but our psyche, having been primed for bribery, was left unutilised, unsatisfied and its thirst for bribery had to be quenched before the festival was over.

We tried all sorts. Bar staff, bar security, back stage security – none of them would go for it. "Twenty pounds to let me to the front of the queue, mate?" Not even a bite. I know I'm a bit tight but… £20!!?

At these festivals the live music stops around 11pm. We had spent a couple of hours with two girls we'd met and wanted to continue drinking back at the campervan. It didn't occur to us that the girls wouldn't be allowed into the campervan field because they didn't have campervan field passes.

The security personnel on the campervan field gate, with their authoritative fluorescent vests and radios, were the law! A more perfect stage for bribery could not have been set. Even Stephen Hawking would be satisfied with the controls built into this experiment.

First we tried charm, flattery and persuasion but to no avail. Then we slipped out a couple of ten pound notes. "Go on mate, no one will mind." Nothing. One guy in particular (we'll call him Mr Block) was a stout professional and stickler for the rules. Nothing would make him waive his responsibilities. He shall perform his duty to his employer, to festival goers, the British public and Her Majesty The Queen come what may. Money or no money, Mr Block wasn't letting these girls, or anyone else, through these gates without a pass.

Instead, Tashy walked through the gates to fetch some beers to drink elsewhere and fortuitously stumbled upon the head of security for the area. Tash regaled his tale of woe including the pitiful, but ultimately victorious line of "do you realise how rarely I get girls back?"

That was what we needed – sympathy! The fella in charge, who was clearly touched by Tash's story, radioed through to allow the girls into the campervan field – *hoorah!* I still remember Mr Block's magnanimous parting remark - "I see you got the better of me."

The friendlier security staff on the gate said later they would have happily let them through but couldn't go against Mr Block. They wouldn't have taken our bribe either but let us through because they couldn't really see the harm in it.

The tragic heroes of this story are Mr Block and the numerous other people who had resisted our attempts to bribe them. I am pleased they did. In fact, it makes me proud of England that none of these people were coerced into breaking the rules for our filthy money.

Furthermore, where people wouldn't bend rules for money, they would if they took pity or because they simply couldn't see the harm in it – a sense of freedom if you like. That was all OK, but any hint of corruption and they would not be party to it. They were all clearly brought up to play with straight bats.

England has its critics. There is much that is not good about England but there is also much that is great. I am pleased to report our rigorous experiment with bribery showed that, in England, it is nigh impossible to find someone who will accept a bribe.

Not so in Sri Lanka. Sri Lankans were falling over themselves to sneak Kish and me into the ground or sell us black market VIP tickets. We had a little chat with a young official on the gate who, for £10 each, gave us a pair of tickets to show to his own security staff and once we had taken a couple of seats (not numbered) he retrieved them from us again. This worked with the ruthless efficiency found only in dark, secret operations. All of this meant that I could watch the day's cricket with Kish which was most enjoyable, and we were in the shade for most of the game.

Sri Lanka had posted a decent score thanks to Jayawardene's 180. Kish, being a big fan of Kevin Pietersen, England's quick scoring, big shot batsman, was very happy to see him come to the crease in England's first innings and happier still to see him leave again a short while later.

By the end of the day both teams had batted; Sri Lanka had a commanding lead but had started poorly in their second innings.

The cricket finished around 4:30pm each day and I would have a much needed shower and perhaps another failed attempt to bend a note on my harmonica before heading out for the sunset around 6pm. Sunset was my favourite time of day in Galle. The temperature drops a little and the sun becomes more sympathetic whilst dyeing the sky a spectrum of reds. I walked around the half a square kilometre of mazy fort area and visited all manner of different places. Not out of choice most of the time; I got lost.

There is a lot to be said for getting lost. Getting lost is the best way to know where you are. A lost person inevitably takes more time to examine their surroundings as they look for clues as to their own whereabouts. I have developed a theory on this that says the learning curve is at its steepest when you know a tiny amount but are otherwise thoroughly ignorant. The more time we spend not knowing where we are, the more we learn about where we are!

I spent a good deal of my early childhood lost; lost in fields, lost in campsites, lost in supermarkets... anywhere I could find. I must have learned loads of stuff. Most memorably, I continuously got lost in our local Asda. My name was frequently called out through the supermarket tannoy system as the helpful staff tried to locate my Mum. By the time I was nine I had a thorough understanding of Asda's lost child procedures and whenever I got lost I would casually walk up to a check out and ask them if they could call my Mum's name over the tannoy system because I'm a lost child. Any child who never got lost in Asda wouldn't have known that.

Losing oneself is also a fine way to find other things. You're sure to leave the beaten track and discover some hidden treasures away from the stage of the main tourist hot spots - some beautiful architecture perhaps or a delightful shop or café; or if you're lucky some unusual people... or eccentric behaviour. It also involves an exciting amount of chance... or risk. How do I get home... and when? For that matter, will I get home? Who lives around here? What's round the next corner? It could be anything, anything at all. It's a gamble and suddenly, just like when we were kids, the possibilities are endless. You could happen upon anything.

I happened upon Copper Steve and his mate, Dave, who took me for a meal at The Peddler's Inn where I nibbled on a delicious, and typically spicy, creamy chicken curry and discovered that a fruit shake is the way to counter the spicy effects. I swear Sri Lankan people have mouths made of asbestos.

I would often walk atop the fort wall to explore the splendid views in the gentle sea breeze. From the west wall one could watch the young lads playing cricket in the coach park before the view stretched into the glistening, sun drenched Indian Ocean beyond. To the South one of the busiest shipping lanes in the world transported cargo around the southern coast of Sri Lanka and off to the Middle East, through the Suez Canal and into Europe. There is always an enormous container ship or two on the horizon. *I wonder how far away the horizon is?* A spattering of small fishing boats and the occasional loitering cruise ship tend to contribute to the view.

Off to the East was the bay which led to Galle Harbour and a noticeable white temple that interrupted the greenery on the other side.

The walk around the fort walls is a very pleasant and peaceful one. The top of the walls are grassy with a stone path that led me almost the entire way round the fort with the highlight of a lighthouse on the east wall where I saw one happy couple get hitched.

Two local daredevils skilfully dived off one of the bastions to the cheers and applause of tourists and school children and then quickly scampered back up the wall to collect donations before the crowd dispersed. The only real interruptions on this gentle stroll came from the occasional toothless bracelet seller, an evening jogger or a crow.

In Sri Lanka crows are everywhere! So far I have seen crows, sparrows and pigeons – hardly what I'd consider exotic. I thought they were restricted to places of bland wildlife like England.

England's wildlife is as dramatic as its weather (Bill Oddy gets overly-excited at seeing a baby blackbird). The best Britain can offer is a grouchy badger. There are many animals in the animal kingdom that are notable for something exciting be it the biggest, fastest, most dangerous, deadliest, biggest teeth, strongest venom, most intelligent, rarest, most colourful, most beautiful, most remarkable in some fashion or other and we provide home for none of them! Perhaps our safety-conscious ancestors shot anything even remotely dangerous or interesting. Even now some people want to continue that less-than-noble tradition by killing badgers and foxes.

My favourite British animal is the otter. The wildlife books I read as a child convinced me that if I popped down to my local stream I could well see a wild otter. In my eighteen years of childhood, and subsequent fifteen years of supposed adulthood I have seen exactly none. I once saw a wild stoat though, ironically, in an otter sanctuary. The little terror was just small enough to creep into the otter's enclosures, relieve them of their lunch, and creep off again. Never trust a stoat.

I spent most sunsets sat on the wall looking out to sea. Everything was so peaceful from the wall. The temperature was perfect, a gentle sea breeze kissed my skin and rippled my hair and the atmosphere was as tranquil as I've ever experienced. If I lived in Galle I would happily sit there at sunset every day.

In that short while, however, the day turns quickly to night. In the short space of half an hour the sun makes way for the stars. On the horizon appeared a score of lights that I hadn't seen before. A local teenager who came to sit with me said they were fishing boats. "They will come in around 5am with their catches," he told me. *I'd like to see that. I'll get up early one morning and watch the sunrise and the fishing boats come in from atop this wall before the heat of the day (and the cricket).* I might as well tell you now that didn't happen, a small regret on my part, but I'm sure it would have been delightful.

This quick sundown nagged at me. *Is it me... am I imagining it? Is it actually going dark quicker? Why would it go dark so quickly?* I sat and conjured a theory that rested blame squarely at the feet of my location on the Earth relative to the equator.

Sri Lanka is close to the Equator, the Earth's fattest point as it spins. Through one spin of the Earth it has to travel much further than, say, the North Pole (which would just rotate on the spot). A bloke stood a metre away from the North Pole will be rotated around the North Pole once, slowly, throughout the day and probably travel about three metres in total. Sri Lanka, at the other extreme, travels the full distance round the Earth, but still in only one day – so travels much faster.

As such, when the sun first touches Sri Lanka's horizon we are travelling so fast that it quickly disappears behind it and gone. I can tell you that if you stand on the Equator you will be travelling at around

1,038 miles an hour. England, some way up in the northern hemisphere, has much less distance to travel during its day, so it travels at a slower speed – around 700 miles an hour. When the sun meets the green hills of our horizon it will still take a couple of hours before it is gone completely. Also, in England the sun crosses the horizon at a diagonal angle which will stretch twilight out a little further.

Also, being so close to the equator means that it goes dark at about the same time of day all year round (in Sri Lanka it ranges from 17:52 to 18:31), and their shortest day of the year, at eleven hours and 43 minutes, is only 48 minutes shorter than their longest day.

So there you have it. Mr Hawking, I hope, will be pleased with that one and it goes down as one of my finer, no doubt already publicly known, theories. I will leave the complex calculations, however, to more thorough men than I.

One other interesting celestial observation I have made whilst on a different part of the Earth is the moon. You will be familiar with the traditional image of the crescent moon and its positioning. When the sun had disappeared below the horizon and the crescent moon stole the attention I noticed it was horizontal - like a smile. The sun went directly below the Earth and shined its light on the moon from underneath. I hadn't really thought of it before but further up the Northern Hemisphere (or down the Southern Hemisphere) the sun is more to the side when below the horizon and generally shines its light on the moon from there.

I found it fascinating to see the sun, moon and earth interact from a different place on the earth. I never dreamt that this trip would give such celestial enlightenment.

Chapter 11 – Galle (Part 2)

From the third morning onwards I woke up wanting to shoot that bloody bird!! If it wasn't for the cricket I would have spent the day hunting it down!

By hook or by crook I had managed to watch the first two days of the cricket inside the ground (alright... entirely by crook) but I watched the rest of the test from the Fort Wall. The Barmy Army had flown their flags, sung and trumpeted from there throughout the first two days and some guys I'd met said the view was fine.

Indeed it was. In fact, better. From the higher vantage point it was much easier to pick out the ball. There was no shade but the sea breeze kept us cool and the views of the ocean and its ships were divine. I picked up something for lunch and some water (as Yorkshire Mick and Karen wisely suggested) and headed over there.

CHRIST ALIVE - A COBRA!!!!! TWO cobras... and a PYTHON!!! Some reckless imbecile had brought his snakes to the cricket! That's NOT playing with a straight bat!

Now, I like to roll dice with Danger from time to time but not with Death, and certainly not with Cobras. This snake exhibitionist had camped up on the path up to the top of the wall. The python was laid out on the concrete looking ill and the two hooded cobras were poking out of their baskets wavering around looking for someone to bite. Suddenly, one of them took a swipe at their 'charmer' who swiftly grabbed the cobra round the neck. *Uurrrrghh, don't do that, man!!*

I have an irrational fear of snakes. Irrational fears are naturally difficult things to figure out... because they're irrational. No doubt some academic folk have written reams to explain the rationale of irrational fears.

My only previous experience of irrational fears was when my Welsh, singing friend Arfon developed an irrational fear of heights. We had flown to Peru, an accomplishment in itself after Arfon had drunkenly sung 'The Wild Rover' to the security staff of Amsterdam's Schiphol Airport as they X-rayed our bags. Whilst exploring the Peruvian mountains Arfon was stopped at a popular tourist path along the edge of a mountain by an intense feeling of vertigo. Dozens of other people were content to walk the path despite its steep descent on one side but no one else caused such fuss. He refused to go on, poor fella. He had not experienced vertigo before and when I asked him what exactly it had felt like he replied, "it's very strange... like I had the sudden urge to jump off!"

My irrational fear, specifically, is that every snake on this fine planet was born with the express purpose of killing me... all of them. It is in their genetic make-up. They just had to find me. In my mind even small, non-venomous snakes would at least have a go if they happened to slither into me.

The species keenest for my murder, however, is the cobra. A more evil creature I could not imagine. The devil himself is in every cobra that ever existed and it chills me to the bone to see them. I'm pretty sure my destiny is, one fateful day, to be killed at the fang of one of these demons.

Rationally, I know that snakes tend to slither away from humans if they hear us coming and don't much fancy a confrontation. Rationally, I am more concerned with the intentions of any bloke wielding a snake than the intentions of the snake itself, but my fear isn't rational.

My fears aren't entirely irrational, either. If I wanted to not be killed by snakes (as I do very much) then Sri Lanka is the first place I shouldn't be. Sri Lanka has the highest death rates by snake bite venom in the world and it's hardly surprising with that mindless buffoon on the fort wall!! Each year 6 people in 100,000 fall dead, victim to snake bites. That's a chance of 1 in 16,666 each year. I have worked out that if a person lives in Sri Lanka for 75 years they have a 1 in only 222 chance of being killed by a snake in their lifetime. My chances, based on these statistics and that I'll be in Sri Lanka for 1 month, are 1 in 200,000 of getting killed by one of these murderous little heathens. I'm sure my chances aren't improved any by our friend with the cobras and the fact that all snakes want to kill me!!

That evening I emailed the whale scientist, Asha de Vos, to see if she might be around to tell me about these blue whales, or even better, take me to see some. It was a long shot I know but, as snooker legend Willie Thorne would say, "it's a shot to nothing". *I wonder what she'll say? I wonder if she'll reply at all.*

Putting the cricket aside for another moment, the fort area at Galle offers some unusual experiences. The place itself reminds me of the old towns in Eastern Europe with its clean, often-cobbled streets with rustic old three-floor buildings. Restaurants, bars, guesthouses and hotels were plentiful, all local and small with friendly, smiley staff.

There were groups (some would say 'hordes') of school children looking very smart in their royal blue shorts and skirts with crisp white shirts. They were generally polite and excitable, especially at seeing foreigners. The brave ones would say 'hi', 'how are you?' or 'which country?' Most would smile. All would stare. On the odd rare occasion a small group would slip out a giggle and look over to me. *Well, if you can't giggle at a 6-foot, clumsy white man, what's the point in being a child?*

Some of them were barefoot and some had shoes. *Why would that be?* I thought. *Is it a money thing, or maybe a comfort thing?* Some of the adults also went barefoot, just walking around the city – no problem.

One morning I chanced upon a school running race on the roads near the cricket ground. The course was marked out with cones and marshalled by stewards. All runners wore running vests in team colours, all had their athlete number pinned onto them and none wore any footwear whatsoever. I watched… and waited… not a single trainer, flip flop or shoe lace amongst them. They must have developed hard skin on the souls of their feet, like I had to get hard skin on my feet to wear my flip flops.

I was further inspired one day on the fort wall. Three girls between sixteen and eighteen or so were shuttle-running along the wall and back again. One girl in mightily impressive form sprinted up and down with enormous gusto whilst wearing a nice, flowery dress and no footwear! I could have married her.

To be able to operate with bare feet all the time sounds like a blissfully comfortable thing. I will make an effort to be barefoot as much as possible to get some hard skin on the souls of my feet – and I did. If I was to walk around my guesthouse, or at the cricket, or in a café, I expelled my flip flops. Sometimes I walked along the fort wall barefoot or even down the street. It felt like a small liberation.

It was surprisingly common for some fella to instigate a chat, maybe talk cricket, or how I like Galle and Sri Lanka. I embraced such opportunities hoping to be rewarded with some unexpected gems of local information. I can tell you that the local tuk tuk driver earns approximately 20,000r a month (£100), one can buy fish in the market and a restaurant will cook it for you and the cash machines around the fort get refilled on Wednesdays so, with the current English occupation, will likely run out by Saturday. One tuk tuk driver I met was desperately looking forward to the day he pays off his tuk tuk.

You might be surprised too at how chatty stiff-looking army officers can be once they begin. One chap was mightily proud to tell me he was a Sergeant and that the heat didn't bother him at all despite his heavy uniforms and exercise drills.

I also learned the interesting point that all these stray dogs that hang around are not stray dogs at all. Most of them 'belong' to someone but not in the way we would think in England. There's no taking the dog for a walk, no leads, no making sure the gate is closed or any of that palaver. The Sri Lankan dog is a free dog! They go where they like, when they like. If they want to go for a walk they take themselves. If they don't, they don't. Presumably the family puts food out and the dog has a sense of belonging but if it didn't like the situation it could leave. This way they all get socialised with other dogs and seem very relaxed.

There is, however, the occasional dog battle over food or girls. It seems non-lethal and perfectly natural. I had one experience late at night when a very angry dog wouldn't let me down his street but other than that these dogs just mope around or join the gang for a prowl around town. I was shocked to witness a dog viciously bite a cat. So it's true that dogs do hate cats after all, or anything that tries to steal away their dinner!

Outside the fort Galle has its fair share of poor people and one such fella followed me. After a bit of the usual chat, 'which country', 'how long in Sri Lanka', this chap offered to take me to a couple of places I might find interesting.

His name, apparently, was Cambridge; a tall, thin, fifty-something with scraggly hair, broken teeth and a very smart pair of trousers (no matter who you meet in Sri Lanka, their plight or their struggles to make ends meet, all the gents can at least manage a smart pair of trousers). Cambridge spoke very good English and was interestingly informative. His wife and two daughters were killed in the 2004 Tsunami – enough to put any man on the back foot.

I took the opportunity to ask him about the local water monitors. "They are very dangerous", he said, and went on to explain that they whip prey and attackers with their tail which is strong enough to break someone's arm.

I found that altogether more believable than the silly nonsense that a swan can break someone's arm with their wing. Surely swan wing bones aren't strong enough. Also, are swans' wing-muscles not built more for endurance than power? Call me a sceptic but that myth sounds like tosh to me. I'm really more interested in what a swan tastes like and why I'm not allowed to eat one. All wild mute swans in the UK are deemed to be the property of Her Majesty the Queen and she won't let us kill and eat them. To be fair I haven't asked her myself, but then she makes herself so very difficult to contact – an astute tactical move on her part.

Geese, ducks, pigeons, grouse and pheasants are all open season and we can buy them very easily, but eat a swan and there would be riots in the streets of Buckingham. I wondered if there is anywhere outside of the UK that happily serves up a roast swan? And what would be the traditional accompaniment? Roast potatoes, carrots, rice? The French don't usually stand in the way of fine cuisine at any cost - perhaps they could help…

Maybe swan is so delicious that they outlawed anyone else to eat it so the Royal family could have the jolly lot to themselves. Or conversely, perhaps swan is terrible. Maybe some King spat out his swan and decided that no one in their right mind would kill a bird so beautiful for a meal so terrible. *Swans should be appreciated in our green lands serenely gliding atop our lakes and rivers, not our dinner tables.* And what sort of King would he be if he were to allow the hard-working yeomen to hunt, kill, prepare and cook swans only to discover them to be utterly disgusting. "No! Swans are off the British menu", declared the good King.

Old Cambridge here had probably never met a swan so I didn't share my swan deliberations with him. Let's get back to the infinitely less graceful water monitor. Once a water monitor has whipped you a few times he might try to bite you, according to Cambridge, and that means serious problems. I felt glad that hissing fella in the drains in Galle retreated back under cover.

"What do water monitors eat, Cambridge?", I asked.
"Dogs!" he replied.
"Dogs!? Really?"
"Yes. Dogs and rotting fish, anything you throw at them." *Oh… hmmm.* What I was getting at was whether they naturally hunt fish or mice or what? Cambridge confirmed that they did. I have to tell you, I'm not sure if Cambridge wasn't just making some of this up.

We were on our way to a crafts shop and passed what looked like a bus stop with people queuing up, mainly women, sitting on chairs on the side of the pavement. It was, in fact, a private doctor's surgery. Cambridge told me how the public hospitals were "not good" so people paid 1,200r (£6) privately just to see a doctor. That doesn't sound much but here you can travel the length of the country or buy an en-suite hotel room for a night for that.

Cambridge introduced me to fish mongers, spice merchants, the crafts shopkeeper and a jeweller. As a naturally tight bloke I was intent on buying nothing but was interested to see the fish for sale, caught that morning in the sea just 20 metres away. The craft shop was actually very impressive; mostly wood carvings that had clearly taken much time, effort and skill. I actually would have bought something if I had been at the end of my travels. The shopkeeper gave me a postcard for free too.

But there was no way I was going to buy anything from the jeweller; an assertion I had previously devised by considering everyone in the jewellery trade to be a crook.

I am completely lost in the world of jewellery and gem stones. To me it is an astounding peculiarity of human beings that we regard gemstones worthy of paying hundreds and thousands of pounds for. You don't see any other mammals engaging in such folly. Were we taught as children that we should really want diamonds and sapphires and be happy to work for days, weeks or even months to obtain just one? Why is it people want them so desperately? Have they not paused to consider why they want them?

I was once shown an impressive diamond ring in Harrods. The charming attendant demonstrated how the diamond split light in several directions casting an even scattering of white dots on her hand. It was quite pretty, admittedly, but not pretty enough to swap £90,000 for, even if it did mean I could see these little dots of light whenever I wanted. The attendant somehow thought me interested enough to give me a copy of the Harrods employee guide to diamonds. My friend Tashy and I were only there trying to find the most expensive item in Harrods.

You'll find me in agreement if you'd like to argue for the unrivalled practical attributes of diamond in the drilling industry, but I'd once again be flabbergasted at the prospect of spending a small fortune on diamond earrings or other such personal decoration. In this, I'm quite sure the world has gone mad.

Still, there are loads of gem shops around, seems to be a bit of a thing round Sri Lanka, so it would be remiss of me not to check one out. With an obvious intention of buying nothing I ambled into the gem shop and bought something. You can imagine my surprise. The whole thing started out as a matter of curiosity – I just wanted to listen to what stream of prattle the salesman would vomit up.

They sit you down and show you lots of different stones in different colours, shapes and sizes. On close inspection some of the colours were very alluring with deep blues and greens and radiant yellows. This jeweller told me the names of them, where they came from and what they could do with them.

"They're all very nice, friend, but I'm not going to buy anything." This was accidental genius. For two minutes I dismissively viewed their wares whilst telling them I wasn't buying. I then realised that a friend's birthday was approaching and spotted a pair of topaz blue earrings that would suit her perfectly. As people in the industry might confirm to you, topaz is not in the same price bracket as diamonds, emeralds or rubies so I was able to bend my usually thrifty rules on this occasion. After unwittingly convincing him that he was wasting his time with me he was thrilled just to make a sale and it was a price so low that it needed his boss's authorisation. *Result!*

The gem shop was the end of my tour with Cambridge. I gave him some money to say thanks and he asked for more so he could buy some food and milk for his kids. *Kids? Not sure that adds up, Cambridge me old mate!!*

Morning started with only a hint of English optimism. After England's dismal first innings where most of our batsmen got out attempting silly sweep shots we were chasing a very challenging target of 340, but having already made 111/2 there was a hint of possibility in the air. To achieve it would be to break England's record for a run chase on this ground but we had a whopping two days at our disposal. The English fans were looking forward with excitement to a slow, patient accumulation of runs; *don't take any risks, no need for big shots, quick scoring or anything remotely flashy or exciting. Take your time fellas,* thought the Barmy Army hoping for a spectacularly dull display of batting. For the England fans to see an exciting end to this game their players were required to play completely unexciting cricket.

I arrived at the fort wall early morning, past those bloody cobras and into the beginnings of a party some opportunistic locals were erecting so they could charge visiting cricket fans an entrance fee to the wall. For this purpose they had supposedly hired this UNESCO World Heritage Site from the powers that be which seemed wholly irregular to me.

I had arrived early enough to catch them on the hop and, as was my tendency in Galle, glided through the gate without paying. A lucky few managed the same until the organisers got their act together. Then, a few more found a sneaky way in round the back until that oversight was addressed too.

In the event the party organisers provided a bar selling reasonably-priced cold beers and dozens of plastic chairs that we wall folk happily commandeered to make ourselves most comfortable for this excitingly dull spectacle of cricket.

A defensive batting stroke that made no attempt to make any runs was well met with hearty cheers and inner contentment, only bettered when no stroke was offered at all. Glorious shots to the boundaries filled the English with anxiety. Ian Bell, a batsman of enviable skill and technique, played a delightful sweep shot that was rewarded with two runs and a shout from a man close to me of "STOP PLAYING BLOODY SWEEP SHOTS!!" *Quite.*

The crowd was comforted to see Jonathon Trott at the crease. If anyone can stand there and resist the urge to entertain it is him. This man has the patience of several saints and loved nothing more than to stand in the middle of a cricket pitch ALL day. Score runs, don't score runs, it all seems the same to him, as long as he's there. Jonathon Trott has his own perception of time. He batted on and on and, with the much quicker scorer Matt Prior at the other end, reduced the target to less than 100 runs needed to win.

Was it a rush of blood, a moment of madness or just reverting to his usual game? Matt Prior dealt with a harmless delivery in his natural fashion – which isn't with a straight bat. The ball was caught at mid-off and his wicket disappeared down the water monitor's drain along with England's chances. The bowlers batted like amateur bowlers and Sri Lanka won a very enjoyable and impressive test match in front of the picturesque fort wall and enthusiastic crowd.

The last day had been very exciting, even if the style of cricket wasn't. Jonathon Trott had slowly reached a century before losing his wicket late in the game and delighted us all with his unwaveringly unadventurous brand of cricket. It was all over and it was only day four.

The day was capped off with a beach party arranged by The Barmy Army at their Hotel in Unawatuna, the beach town just a few minutes' tuk tuk ride along the south coast. They did a grand job. After making a charitable donation for entry of 1,000r (£5), drinks were very reasonably priced and there were five bars to choose from along with a BBQ, fast food counter, highlights of the cricket on the big screen and entertainment.

That Barmy Army trumpeter joined a band on stage for a version of 'Give it Up' by KC and the Sunshine Band. The band bashed out a whole bunch of tunes before they conducted a raffle and an auction for signed cricket memorabilia from the England Cricket team. I found a Barmy Army stall and couldn't resist buying a Barmy-Army-on-tour-in-Sri Lanka polo shirt to remember my first cricket tour by. If all of this wasn't enough Jonathon Agnew, the well-respected BBC radio commentator, turned up to talk cricket with anyone who wanted to.

After a couple of chats with people I had met around the fort I must admit to feeling a little lonesome. I had hoped Copper Steve and Dave might show up having tipped me off about the party. I soaked up the atmosphere for a while with a casual beer as my only company. Everyone else had come in groups and specifically for the cricket where as I was on my own, sneaking the cricket into a much larger expedition.

After a while I duly left, on my own, and went to bed. *Tomorrow is the fifth day of the test but as it's finished already, what will I do?*

Chapter 12 – Galle Day Off

I had walked the fort walls and been lost and found in the streets of the fort countless times. I'd been all round the cricket ground and had ventured into the new town with Cambridge. The one other thing that had caught my imagination was the view of the harbour and the great ships docked in it so I set off to have a closer look.

With time on my hands I walked towards the harbour and looked for the entrance to the harbour. What I found was a tall iron gate and a couple of armed guards. *Blast!!* It turned out this harbour is an International Port and Navy Base and, as such, is protected by heavy security. *Blast!!* "Authorised Personnel" doesn't include an ambling, curious Englishman looking for some amusement. My plan was foiled.

Wait a minute! I spotted a narrow lane next to the gate that skirted round the side of the harbour. *Maybe there's a spot where I could at least get a close view of the harbour and those huge, docked tankers.* There were no signs explaining what was down this lane or that I wasn't allowed to wander down it… so down it I went.

What else was I going to do with my day? I was looking for inspiration so it made sense to follow a whim and to take my time about it. This is one of the many unmerited benefits of the much maligned, dark art of inefficiency.

Inefficiency's good-looking and charming elder brother, Efficiency, almost always wins the plaudits in this fast-paced, ordered world, but Inefficiency also has much to offer. For instance, a swimmer blessed with Inefficiency, swimming with arms and legs ungainly scattered all over the place, will burn off more calories over a length of the pool than a swimmer cursed with Efficiency. I ask you, who has had the more successful work out?

The training regimes of elite athletes are built on Inefficiency. Linford Christie, Britain's fastest ever sprinter, famously used to run whilst dragging a tractor tyre behind him, and many top athletes train at high altitude to increase the inefficiency of absorbing oxygen. Their performance is improved as a result.

Inefficiency has its glamorous side too. Consider the shiny sports cars that adorn the driveways of the rich and wasteful. The Bugatti Veyron 16.4 Grand Sport Vitesse operates at an average of only 10 miles per gallon and sells at a very uneconomical $2million; and for all that fuel and money it can still only transport 2 people – drastically inefficient. Inefficiency is the core principle of its design and, as such, regarded as one of the most thrilling, sensational and prestigious vehicles obscene volumes of money can buy.

Nature's most inefficient members are also its most exciting. The cheetah burns away copious amounts of valuable energy by running at speeds up to 100 km/h; and elephants are known to consume 200 kilos of vegetation and 200litres of water every day.

Compare the thrilling and dramatic reputations of those magnificent beasts to that of the super-efficient three-toed sloth, an animal reputed to be so filthy it has been found in outdoor camp toilets gorging on human excrement; and their hair typically accommodates two or three species of algae, a hundred moths, a thousand beetles and plenty more ticks.

As far as mammals go, the three-toed sloth cannot be beaten for its efficiency. They somehow manage to survive for an average of 20 years in the wild on only a scrap of energy they glean from their usual diet of leaves. To keep energy expenditure down the three-toed sloth sits in its tree perfectly still for twenty hours a day… absolutely motionless… and only goes to the toilet once a week (one of the rare few times they leave their tree). On the infrequent occasions they are inclined to travel they are gradual, though when fleeing from immediate danger they can achieve speeds of up to four metres a minute.

These hairy bundles of inactivity further save energy by maintaining the lowest body temperature of all mammals and retaining only a quarter of the muscle mass of similar sized mammals. They are weak, undramatic and uninspiring. I dare say you will never see an American Football team called the New York Three-Toed Sloths, though I would love it if we did.

These are fine arguments, I'm sure you'd agree, but even they shrink to insignificance next to Inefficiency's greatest achievement – the advancement and diversity of life. DNA replicates itself with mind-blowing Efficiency but it is the infinitesimally small involvement of Inefficiency that has allowed life-forms to change, grow and improve in millions of ways over millions of generations.

The first entity of life, probably a molecule or set of molecules that could replicate itself, relied upon Inefficiency to replicate itself imperfectly so that its descendants were bigger, stronger, more complex and generally better.

Granted, he hasn't always got it right; really he just throws ideas out and lets natural selection decide whether they are any good or not – but the positive changes can last for millions of years. Inefficiency, inefficiently sprinkled throughout the three and a half billion years of life, has sparked the development of the millions of different species of animal, plant, fungi, single celled organisms and micro-organisms that we see today... and he hasn't finished yet. Inefficiency will be altering life wherever he can find DNA replication to meddle with long after us Homo sapiens have disappeared. He may even be the cause of that.

Efficiency is always much too busy churning stuff out to stand back and try new things. He doesn't see the point. Such silliness is just wasting time that could have been better spent churning more stuff out. Where Efficiency is the brother of building, replicating and producing, Inefficiency is an ideas man, spending his time slumped, half-drunk in the corner of a dingy boozer talking gibberish, dreaming up daft notions and blurting out the occasional idea that changes the world.

I first began to develop my own skills in inefficiency just after University. I did happen to display a certain flair for it at University but it was when my good friend Basil and I started office temp jobs that we made rapid progress. Spending our days at different companies, our temp jobs required us to do almost no work. Once the work was done we would seek more work, read information that was much too dull to commit to memory or find anything to avoid doing nothing. Once all avenues were exhausted the day would drag, the mood would slip and there was a very real danger of entering into a type of hell that closely resembled the Sri Lankan Department of Immigration. The problem was boredom and the only remaining solution to this most torturous of circumstance was Inefficiency.

Basil and I would take all the tasks that needed to be done, however small, and take as long as possible about them. The more accustomed approach of speed and efficiency didn't apply. Why use copy and paste when you can spend time typing words out manually – maybe improving one's typing at the same time? Why phone someone else in the building when you can go and see them... a good four floors away?

The aim was partly to *stretch* activity but chiefly to *create* activity, however pointless. It can be a turbulent internal process, to resist all of the time-saving techniques that have been programmed and ingrained into each of us from childhood, but the field of Inefficiency is relatively untapped so there is plenty to be discovered.

Inefficiency can spread like wildfire. I would fetch and drink lots of water. The more water I drank the more I would have to go to the toilet. And heaven forbid I would go to the toilet AND fetch water on the same journey. Nor would I go the shortest route. Why not walk the path less travelled – who knows what more Inefficiencies I might find on the way. It's thinking in a completely different way and soon you realise the possibilities are endless.

Never begin any task of significance without making a cup of tea first; and if I was making myself a cup of tea I might as well make everyone a cup of tea. Very efficient for everyone else; tremendously inefficient for me.

The most celebrated accomplishment was to invent a brand new inefficiency. With such an innovation came an activity triple-whammy effect. First was the inefficiency itself. Second was the inefficiency of us both discussing the inefficiency at length and third was the inspirational effect on the other to double his efforts to also invent a brand new inefficiency. It was like a self-reproducing organism.

Technology was a dreadful hindrance. Photocopiers could copy hundreds of sheets of paper with only 2 pushes of buttons; one e-mail could go to any number of people at once and spreadsheets were horrendous – one of the least inefficient tools found in the modern office. They made typing virtually redundant. A task that might previously have taken up to half a day could now be completed inside of a minute.

Despite all of this, Inefficiency has somehow acquired an unfavourable reputation. I'll admit he is not always the go-to man when one embarks on a mission but everyone and everything has their strengths and weaknesses. Lionel Messi is generally regarded as the best footballer in the world but you wouldn't put him in goal.

Inefficiency is the unsung hero that grafts inefficiently only to watch his name be dragged through the mud by people who haven't taken the trouble to understand him. He has achieved a great many things and suffers, in the public eye, in the euphoria surrounding his glamorous brother, Efficiency. His is a thankless task but he does it consistently and with stubborn resolve all over the world in countless different HR departments.

Curious Chronicles from Sri Lanka

With my old friend Inefficiency, I followed the lane towards the sea and slightly uphill into some green and leafy grounds that stopped at a cliff. There was a view point at the edge of the cliff, a circular, stone Gazebo with a pillar in the middle supporting a circular bench and a roof that gave shelter from the beating sun. It was the perfect place for rest and water whilst taking in the ocean view.

Similar to the view from the fort wall, I looked out across the Indian Ocean to the southern horizon. I was at the midpoint of the bay between Galle Fort and Unawatuna on a piece of land that jutted out only slightly into the bay. There was a curved beach on my left (east side) that was hidden to the fort wall and beyond that was the far peninsula with the noticeable white temple.

I reclined and enjoyed a good close up view of the harbour on the right with its battered old ships, tankers, fishing boats and cruise ship - the best view I was going to get.

I again wondered how far it was to the horizon, a question that I have often wondered since I first looked out to sea as a child. I can't measure it but there must be a way of calculating it. Perhaps I could figure it out with some paper, a pen, a calculator, some intermediate mathematics and enough time. I had with me my diary and pen, an out-of-date A-level in mathematics, a rudimentary calculator on my cheap phone and ALL DAY, so I set to work.

The horizon is the edge of the Earth that I can see – the curvature of the Earth makes the Earth beyond disappear below the horizon, so the distance to the horizon will vary depending on how high up I am. I drew a section of the curved Earth and a small cliff with me on top. I then drew a line, my line of sight, from my eye to the horizon – a straight line that clipped the edge of the curved Earth marking the point of the horizon.

The first important mathematical concept to involve is that the straight line from my eye to the horizon is a tangent to the Earth which means that, if the Earth is a perfect sphere, it will form a right angle with the line from the horizon to the Earth's centre. The length of that line is the radius of the Earth (r) which we can find out in due course. If I draw a second line from the centre of the Earth to my eye the length will be the radius of the Earth plus how high up I am ($r + h$). It looked like this:

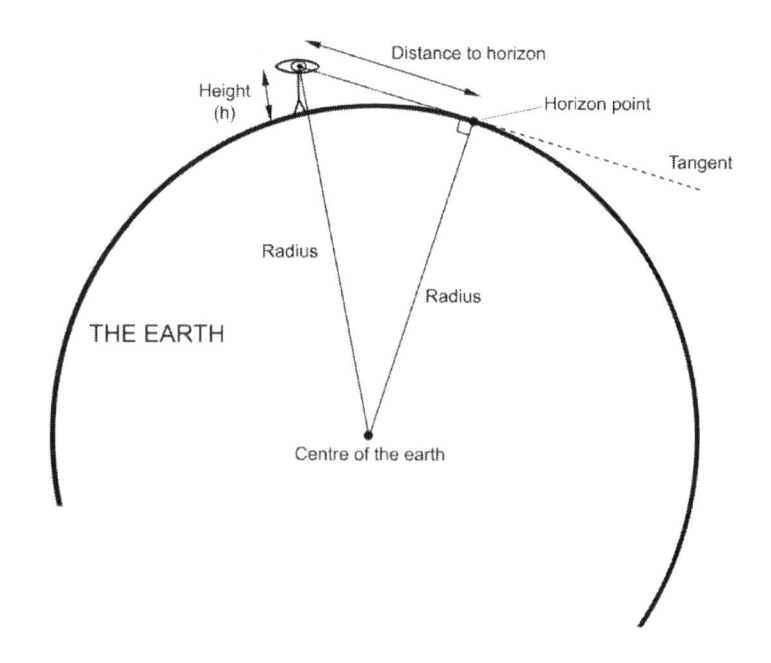

Diagram: Cross-section of the Earth showing a person of Height (h) standing on the surface, with lines indicating the Distance to horizon, Horizon point, Tangent, two Radius lines meeting at the Centre of the earth, labelled THE EARTH.

So, with that right-angled triangle this thing should be possible somehow, but I still needed to know the radius of the Earth. If I knew the circumference of the earth I could work it out with that most round of numbers, 3.142......, pi.

As I was pondering this problem a tall, middle-aged French man marched into view with a group of young adults. "Hello!" he cried to me theatrically, and on seeing me engrossed with paper and pen enthusiastically added, "What are you doing?" *Oh no, this is embarrassing.*

"Hi!! Erm... I was just wondering how far it is to the horizon... so I'm trying to work it out." *Christ! I wonder what he'll think to that.*

"Ahh, let me see" he keenly blasted again. "Ah, yes, perhaps trigonometry." I explained to this zealous Frenchman that I was thinking that maybe Pythagoras could solve this. He reviewed my diagram again. "Yes! Very good, you can work it out from that, I think," and with that he advanced to the edge of the cliff to inspect the view.

I chanced my arm. "Excuse me", I called out to anyone who was prepared to listen. "... er... does anyone happen to know the circumference of the Earth?"

"Forty thousand kilometres", replied a French girl instantly. A little startled and impressed, I thanked her kindly. It turned out this was a group of geography students on a study trip from Paris. The excitable middle-aged gent was their lecturer.

An attractive, red haired girl called Laura sat next to me and took an interest in my small horizon project. "I would love to travel alone", she said. "It must be amazing to zust go where you want and when you want. We have to go where zey tell us. Zere is a… er… schedule?"
"Yes, schedule. It must be fun travelling with your friends though?" I offered.
"It is fun but we 'ave no freedom. We cannot explore like you are doing."
"I must say, it is great to travel independently and explore… but sometimes I get a bit lonely and do silly things like calculate the distance to the horizon." She laughed, to my amazement.

The Frenchman was lecturing on the edge of this cliff with wild animation and spirited gestures. "What is he saying?" I asked Laura.
"He says… zis bay on zer left was made by a meteor hitting ze Earth… many years ago, or so zey zink." *Well, what do you know?* I had sat in the ideal place to observe a meteor site of geographical significance. I had never knowingly seen a meteor site before. *How marvellous.*

As quickly as the French had stormed my gazebo… they left and traipsed off towards their bus. An all-too-fleeting a visit unfortunately but I was pleased they dropped by. *Oh well, now where was I? Pythagoras, I think.* I found my page again thinking it a shame that I wouldn't see Laura or the lecturer again.

Five minutes later I looked up to see Laura stood in front of me. "Hi", she said. "I hope you don't zink zis is…er… weird… er… have you ever been to Paris? I mean, I can show you if you want to see it", she said handing me her phone number. "Paris is a beautiful city" she said "and you would enjoy it more if I showed you. I am free a lot, very free, so you should come." *Ooh la la!!*

Don't worry, this book isn't going to transform into a romantic novel, more's the pity. As it was I had plans to be in Asia for the next two months. I told her that I would love to and she left… again.

Right! I resolved. Never mind the charms of this enchanting young French girl, what of this horizon formula? Firstly, if the circumference of the Earth is 40,000km (or 40,000,000 metres) then, using the formula C = 2 r pi, I calculated that the radius of the Earth is 6,365,372 metres.

Pythagoras found that, for a right angle triangle, the square of the two shorter sides would equal the square of the longest side. So…

short side² + other short side² = Longest side² , or to apply it to the horizon

distance to horizon² + earth radius² = (earth radius + height)²

After inserting a few symbols to tidy up such as d = distance to horizon, r = radius of the earth and h = height above sea level, and some algebraic jiggery-pokery, we get;

d = √((r + h)² − r²)

or

d = √((6,365km + h)² − 40,513,225km)

This formula is the important part of all this as it allows us to calculate with very good accuracy the distance to the horizon from whatever height we choose. Let's try it from 15 metres up.

d = √((6,365km + 0.015km)² − 40,513,225km²)

d = 14km roughly

So, when looking out to sea from 15 metres above sea level the horizon is about 14km away. Also, at 2 metres high, as if I was standing on the beach, the horizon would be about 5km away.

I must tell you that this is only a very close estimate, mainly because the earth isn't actually a perfect sphere. Even if we ignore land irregularities like mountains it is still not a sphere for two reasons. First, and most important, the Earth's spin causes the Oceans to bulge around the equator and secondly, the ocean tides created by the moon's gravity create temporary variations in the curvature of the Earth. In fact, the Earth's radius at any given point ranges between 6,353km and 6,384km, less than 0.5% difference. I will leave the calculations of that to more meticulous scientists and mathematicians than I. If that is you, do let me know how this would affect my horizon formula (many thanks).

I have subsequently discovered that this method was created and used in reverse by a chap called Al-Biruni from what is now Uzbekistan.

With help from a large lake he used it to calculate the radius of the Earth back in the very early 11th century.

You may think that they didn't know the Earth was round in the 11th century but the idea that the earth was a sphere has been around for millennia well before Al-Biruni, but recorded evidence and published work from back then are a little sparse. The myth that people thought the Earth was flat, from my bit of research, applied to only a small section of society. Other sections knew it to be spherical while various others theorised it to be a disc, a dome, a cylinder and some crazy Egyptian monk called Cosmas thought it was a flat parallelogram!

We only started attaining evidence, as Stephen Hawking mentions in his book, when the great Italian astronomer Galileo Galilei, born in the 16th century, surmised that the Earth was a sphere when he observed many lunar eclipses. When the Earth gets directly between the sun and the moon it casts its shadow on the moon. If the Earth was any other shape than a sphere then the shadow on the moon would have shown different shapes, at least some of the time, but it is always round.

If we could come back to Sri Lanka, my old friend Inefficiency and I made a good breast it. From wandering down that lane on a whim we developed a formula to accurately estimate the distance to the horizon if one's height above sea level is known. We viewed the harbour, saw the site of a meteor crash, met a French geography class and were invited to Paris by a lovely young woman.

I'd wager I had a better day with Inefficiency than I would have had with that pompous, glorified creep, Efficiency. Efficiency and I would have likely motored along, successfully racking up the miles, ticking off sights, meeting deadlines, beating targets, having our backs patted by Senior Management and spending the entire day in near misery.

Happy with my day's work I found my way back to the Admiral's house and his butler. The butler's three children had come to visit though still no sign of the Admiral, but I had a bit of fun with the kids, tea and cake with the butler and a more coherent chat. The Admiral, he tells me, is an advisor to the President. He spends most of his time in Colombo... advising, though I'm not sure what about.

Funnily enough the next morning, as I sat on the fort wall for the last time, I received a text message. It was from "PRESIDENT", it said. *How did he get my number?* On opening the text I read that the President of Sri Lanka was inviting me to join him (along with everyone else) the following day in celebrating Earth hour - an hour in which we all turn off our lights to remind ourselves to save power. Most Sri Lankans I spoke to thought this was just a move by the government to save on power because they regularly run out and suffer power cuts. Still, what a novel way of communicating with the people; never let it be said that the Sri Lankan Government isn't embracing technology.

    I left Galle for Unawatuna with my text message from the president, wondering if it had been sent under the advice of the Admiral...

Chapter 13 – Unawatuna

Because there's nothing to do but layabout or surf, Unawatuna is a small popular tourist town for layabouts and surf bums. It lies further along the coast behind the peninsula with the glowing white temple and is primarily an idyllic banana-shaped beach lined with palm trees, guesthouses and fine restaurants with fine lobster.

I poked my head into the kitchen of one such restaurant to address the chef. "Hi, will you have lobster on tonight?" I asked.
"Lobster?" he confirmed. "You want opium?"
"Er... no... lobster, please", I requested.
"Yes, we have lobster... and opium."
"Istudee (thank you)." *What an obliging fella.*

Unawatuna isn't a place for deep exploration, the adventure is over in thirty minutes. It is a place to exist and, if you have the energy, ponder a while. As it happens Unawatuna is a fitting place to think about physics.

It is casually assumed that the strength of Earth's gravity is the same all over the planet, but I can tell you it isn't. The Earth's density is variable all around the planet creating slight changes in the gravitational force and, it is rumoured, you would be at your lightest in Unawatuna. If our opium chef weighs 60Kg in England then in Unawatuna he would weigh 59.9Kg.

On 11 Nov 2013 a news story described how the GOCE space satellite had free fallen to Earth, as planned, after exhausting its fuel supply. Launched into orbit in 2009 one of its missions was to finely measure and map gravitational variations around the globe which it happily accomplished in blistering form before plummeting unceremoniously to its retirement (total destruction) in the South Atlantic Ocean.

The single most dramatic aspect of its findings is that Unawatuna, Sri Lanka in general and a large section of the Indian Ocean south of Sri Lanka has the lowest gravitational pull on the planet, in comparative terms by some measure.

No one really knows why this is. Nevertheless, some imaginative folk suggest that this makes Sri Lanka the best place in the world from which to launch rockets into space and, as a nation, they might make a handsome fortune by marketing themselves to the world's space agencies.

It too has been identified, for similar reasons, to be the place most likely chosen for an approach by visiting aliens. A variation in the gravitation pull of 0.015% compared to the average would apparently make all the difference. I wondered if the abundance of whales, a species known mostly for its great weight, was in anyway linked to this gravitational low spot - a new area of research for some budding young scientist perhaps.

It also occurred to me that this variation in the earth's gravitational pull would have an impact, however small, upon the distance to the horizon. I would expect the ocean to cling to the Earth less and perhaps bulge ever-so-slightly in these areas affecting the curvature of the Earth. A more dedicated individual than I might like to look into that and factor the effect of this variable into my horizon equation.

The strongest gravitational force on the planet, incidentally, is at the north and south poles and a large area including and surrounding Papa New Guinea. The UK and western European countries have a particularly strong gravitational force too making us that little bit heavier than virtually everyone else.

With the sound of the ocean close by, the warm evening air caressing my skin, the stars sparkling in the heavens and the lobster thermidor residing happily in the belly, the scene was set for an evening with Stephen Hawking.

Hawking explains how there are now two sets of laws of physics, the classical laws for the normal, recognisable world, and quantum physics for the very small. To us quantum physics is a confusing business. The first thing to understand about quantum physics is that if you think you understand it you probably don't understand it. It includes particles popping in and out of existence and instantaneously affecting other particles light years away, just as a taster. Such is the "exotic" nature of quantum physics it describes a particle travelling from A to B on a number of different paths all at once.

The behaviour of the particle can be as erratic, bizarre and irregular as even our most wild minds could imagine and is impossible to predict with total certainty, but when in large groups the average of their behaviours is what we recognise in our everyday lives. The air in a room at 20°C is full of particles at different temperatures but the average of them is 20°C. It may be that a particle exactly at the average of 20°C doesn't exist.

To my mind Newton's three laws of motion, that satisfactorily explains how forces interact with recognisable objects, does little to help us understand the behaviour of particles, They are really more trends of a collection of particles than actual laws.

It turns out that Niels Bohr in his 'Correspondence Principle', first used in 1913, says that the laws of quantum physics (the behaviour of a particle) produce the trends that we recognise in classical physics when dealing with a large number of particles. So, although we understand and can predict how the group behaves, the single particle can still do lots of eccentric stuff that we can't predetermine.

The same, I'd suggest, is true of people. People's behaviour can be so wonderfully "exotic" we can't predict with certainty what an individual will do. We can gather information, look at trends, put people in groups and classifications and attach probabilities, but still not be able to predict, with certainty, what the individual will do.

A neutron, however couldn't care less if it gets thrown together with another billion neutrons to be assumed as identical despite their individual behaviours - it isn't affronted when it finds itself at the sharp end of injustice, the thin end of unfairness or the ugly end of an insult. But a person is likely to take considerably greater exception to having their individual merits and rights ignored and assumed to be exactly the same as everyone else in a group they have been assigned to.

Even so, the modern world is still full of examples where, in trying to understand an individual, a huge group of other people is evaluated. Consider the absurdity of a young lad applying for car insurance and the insurance company assigns a judgement to him by assessing the behaviour of a bunch of *other* young lads. Actually different people! This, of course, is the basis of prejudice.

A more complicated and even less useful analysis of an individual is the psychometric test which, by one of these mind-boggling quirks of human society, appears to be growing more common. I have recently had the intense displeasure of completing one. It entailed answering some 250 questions with either a 'yes' or 'no' answer, and someone who I've never met claimed to be able to determine my personality and suitability for a specific job.

It asked 'do you like loud parties?' and 'did you get into trouble at school?' and 'do you talk a lot in social situations?' and 'do you like meeting new people?' Presumably Mr Psychologist used formulae that attempted to interpret my answers to reveal personality traits incorporating psychological theories and the answers gathered from a whole load of other, different people. No doubt he'd have my personality mapped out on an Excel spreadsheet.

The whole thing seems wildly unreliable for lots of reasons; the complete boredom and indifference of the person questioned, the huge potential for misinterpreting the meaning of answering 'yes' or 'no' to questions that ordinarily require a more detailed response or deliberate manipulation of answers to arrive at the desired result. The reasons behind answers might be wholly different to anticipated reasons behind answers with the inevitable compounded inaccuracies of scores, weightings and other artificially quantified results. How can you reliably score leadership skills or creativity?

Is it more relevant that I like loud parties or that I got into trouble at school when determining my personality? (Although, I only like loud parties from time to time and usually only if I know quite a few people there and if the music is good. Usually I prefer a nice sit down round a table in a pub with good friends and good beer, although I do like meeting new people… and I only got into a bit of trouble at school like most people - just talking or making a joke or experimenting with the gas taps in Science but a couple of times I did rebel at some injustice.) All Mr Psychologist can ascertain from a 'yes' answer to liking loud parties is that I like loud parties, even though, quite often, I don't.

In the event Mr Psychologist concluded that I would be a good leader – of course he did. I answered it so that he would. The other insight he offered was that I'm confident in situations I know about and less confident in situations I don't. *Genius!* I am told Mr Psychologist received good money for this deduction.

There is a lot more activity putting numbers on things you can't put numbers on going on in the world. People are trying to measure the financial value of confidence, put a number on effective group dynamics and a score on a relationship. In this I am in accord with that great man, Albert Einstein, who so wisely said, "Not everything that counts can be counted, and not everything that can be counted counts."

Whilst reading Hawking's book and letting my mind wander it occurred to me that everything in the universe that hasn't been designed has come to be what it is through evolution. The effects of time and chance has, depending on your beliefs, shaped the Earth, the life-forms on it, the stars and the galaxies.

Could it be that, in that brief time that followed the big bang, the laws of physics themselves have too suffered the process of evolution and *evolved*? Could it be that, at a speed known only to the oldest components of the universe and the Sri Lankan Department of Immigration, they could still be evolving?

The next morning I awoke early to embark on an adventurous walk along a jungle path I found heading along the coast towards Galle and its cash machines. Through peaty smelling brush I strolled along some almost forgotten path, the unruly jungle vegetation spilling over providing glimpses of shade from the warming sun. I met exactly zero people on this walk. I clambered over a few wire fences until the path delivered me to that glowing white temple I had seen from Galle's fort walls and up to the main road back to Galle.

At the cash machine just inside the fort a forty something, well groomed and confident English bloke queued in front of me while his wife / girlfriend / whatever waited in the car. "How much do we need, honey?" he shouted to his partner.

"Get 10,000 rupees", she shouted back.

"May I make a suggestion", I interjected. "If you get 9,900 rupees it will give you some small notes too. You know what it's like round here for change."

"Hey, that's a really good idea." he beamed.

"Also, make sure you get enough. They only refill the machines on Wednesdays so it's likely to run out soon, what with all the cricket fans around."

He returned to his car to explain to his partner why he'd withdrawn 14,900 rupees and I began my journey to Mirissa feeling more confident that I was beginning to get a handle on things out here.

Chapter 14 – Mirissa and Blue Whales

Having survived the reckless whims of three bus drivers I finally made it to Mirissa, Sri Lanka, the inspiration behind this whole trip and home to blue whales… so what about them?

As the biggest animal on Earth they have been known to grow up to 33 metres long and weigh over 180 tonnes, although accurately weighing a blue whale is more than a bit tricky. Blue whales in the northern hemisphere ordinarily grow to 25 metres whilst those in the Southern hemisphere generally grow to 30 metres. Its tongue is as big as an elephant, its heart weighs in at some 600kg and it is said that small children can crawl through its arteries, which I hope never happens.

It is too difficult to reliably determine with any sort of accuracy how many blue whales are swimming around the world, especially as they tend to sail the oceans alone or with just their young calf. We're certain there are a lot fewer than there were 100 years ago, before the whale hunters killed around 390,000 of them. Blue whales are good for their oil, amongst other things, and they were hunted to near extinction until whaling was banned in 1986. Scientists think there are anywhere between 5,000 and 15,000 left but there is no way to know for sure.

Blue whales eat almost nothing but krill (tiny shrimp-like creatures). Where you might expect them to have teeth they instead have baleen plates that act as filters. By opening their wide mouths they scoop up their own body weight of water and whatever is in it and then squeeze the water back out through these baleen plates trapping all the krill, and the occasional small fish, squid or crustacean, inside.

One of the biggest mysteries about the blue whale is how and why they communicate. You'll probably know that they communicate by sound and most scientific discussion includes theories that 'singing' is for attracting mates, forming navigational maps, finding food or each other and identifying one another.

The blue whale is phenomenally loud. They are one of the loudest animals on Earth and we can't hear them at all. They 'sing' at such a low pitch that the human ear is unable to pick it up. Whale acoustics researcher, Mark MacDonald, was trying to track the movements of blue whales by listening to their singing and accidentally discovered that their average pitch may have lowered as much as half an octave since the 1960's. He found himself regularly re-calibrating his machines to listen for ever-decreasing frequencies and realised that this in itself could be of significance. It was subsequently found that blue whales worldwide were singing at lower frequencies, although to a varying amount.

John Hildebrand of Scripps Oceanography believes this may be a sign that blue whale numbers are increasing, or so the theory goes...

The males sing to attract the females. The bigger the whale the lower they can sing and, to the females of the species, size matters. So the males deliberately try to sing as low as possible to impress the females with their size, but they have a trade-off to consider. By singing at a lower pitch their sound won't carry as far through the water so would reach fewer females. *Do you chance your arm with as many females as possible or concentrate your efforts? A question many a man has considered.*

John Hildebrand theorises that if blue whales are spread more thinly they have to sing at higher frequencies to reach the nearest whale. Therefore, their lowering of frequency over the last fifty years or so may be because they don't need their song to travel as far, indicating that there are more whales around.

Other theories for why they sing lower involve the rising temperature or acidity of the sea and the increase of human industry in the sea, the noise of which obscures the sounds from the whales, but these theories have problems with them. The shift in sea temperature and acidity is not thought to be nearly enough to require the amount of pitch change scientists have observed, and if the whales needed to cut through the industrial noises they would do better to sing at higher frequencies, not lower.

An exciting theory of my own devising is that now the whales are not being killed all the time they are growing older and bigger on average and are more able to sing at lower frequencies as each year goes by. Incidentally, male blue whales also show off by singing a note for as long as possible to show that they can take in more air, again suggesting to listening females that they are bigger.

My research into blue whales' singing led to a chap called Roger Bland, a professor of physics at San Francisco State University in California, who found that all of the blue whales in a single population sing at near-exactly the same pitch. His research into a population off the coast of California measured the whales to sing at, or extremely close to, 16.02Hz (or four octaves below middle C). Firstly, this shows that they are acutely aware of pitch and, secondly, able to produce the pitch they'd like with stunning accuracy.

They think the whales sing at the same pitch to find each other by using the same technique that Hubble used to discover the Universe was accelerating in its expansion - the Doppler Effect. Similar to an ambulance siren as it hurtles past - the pitch of the sound created doesn't change but the pitch the listener hears changes depending on whether the source of the sound (the ambulance) is travelling towards the listener or away. Whales swimming away from the source would hear a pitch lower than 16.02Hz, as the sound waves are stretched, and slightly higher than 16.02Hz if swimming towards the source and the sound waves are compressed. As such, they can figure out which way to swim to find the singing whale.

Almost every blue whale in the world's great oceans spends most of its time travelling from one area on Earth to another. They find it necessary to give birth in the comfortable warm waters close to the equator and, as a cruel matter of fate, find food in abundance in the nutrient-rich and very cold waters of the Arctic and Antarctic. As such they are forced to swim regular, lengthy and dangerous migrations.

The population of blue whales living just off the south coast of Sri Lanka, however, has managed to cheat the cruel trickery of the fates. There, they have found the continental shelf where the ocean descends very deep very quickly. The meeting of the warmer coastal waters with the colder waters of the continental shelf creates a cycle of rising nutrients. The rich, rotting matter from the ocean bed feeds the krill, and the krill feed the whales. This population of whales lives in their warm waters with an abundance of food only a five minute dive away. They are perhaps the luckiest bunch of whales on Earth and the only population known to us to stay in the same place all the time. For this reason Asha de Vos calls them the 'Unorthodox Whales'.

After the end of Sri Lanka's civil war in 2009 boats were allowed back onto the sea and it is only then that this population of blue whales was discovered. The scientific research and whale watching industry in this area is in its infancy.

This area also happens to be home to spinner dolphins, giant mantas and SPERM WHALES!!! Sperm whales, with the huge box-shaped heads and made famous by Moby Dick, are particularly exciting. They are one of the larger whales, measuring up to 20 metres, but their behaviour is totally different to the blue whales.

Sperm whales tend to live in large groups called 'pods' and have very strong bonds with each other; mothers are happy to leave their calves under the protection of other pod members while they hunt. It appears the sperm whales close to Sri Lanka form 'super-pods' of over forty individuals.

Furthermore, where you might have expected baleen plates, they have very large teeth and are hunters of the humboldt squid, giant squid and the colossal squid found at the bottom of deep oceans (as well as smaller marine life). They have been known to dive for up to 90 minutes and over 3km deep (the bottom of the continental trench off Sri Lanka is around 2.5km deep). The mystery with sperm whales is what it is they're doing down there...

Generally, they dive deep to catch giant squid but *how* do they catch their giant squid? There are theories, of course. *Hooray!!* The first, and generally accepted, aspect is that their huge heads house echolocation equipment enabling them to find their prey in the dark depths of the ocean. Similar to bats, they send out sounds or 'clicks' that hit objects and bounce back to the whale (an echo) allowing them to work out how far away an object is and, often, what it is.

Then, so one exciting theory goes, they can produce and direct sound clicks so intense (the loudest sound made by any animal) that they can render a giant squid unconscious. *What an extraordinary weapon.* So extraordinary that it's probably not true at all.

Since this theory was put forward some scientists have blasted squids with intense bursts of sound to see if this could indeed stun the poor critter. They made the remarkable discovery that not only did the sound bursts fail to stun the squid, the squid weren't affected in the slightest. They remained blissfully oblivious of the whole experiment regardless of how many sonic blasts were thrown at them.

Based on this evidence the experiment concluded that squid are deaf which brings a different relevance in terms of sperm whale attacks. The clicks required for echolocation could ordinarily be heard by the prey, betraying the predator's whereabouts, but the deaf squid are seemingly susceptible to having sperm whales sneak up on them undetected. A scary thought indeed.

Another clue to the sperm whale's hunting practices was recently obtained. In 2010, the excellently named Bruce Mate, director of Oregon State University's Marine Mammal Institute in Newport, tagged a bunch of sperm whales with global positioning systems and ultimately found that they tend to hunt in teams. They tagged three sperm whales in a pod and found that one whale would often dive much deeper than the other two. Scientists speculate that they were herding the squid together making them easier to snatch with the deeper whale cutting off an escape route to unreachable depths.

This technique has been observed in sea lions, dolphins and other whales in environments a little easier for human access. They also found that the deep diving role was rotated between the whales. This is consistent with physiological evidence that very deep dives are stressful to the sperm whale and takes its toll on their bodies, though I also suspect the different roles achieve varying amounts of dinner. Ultimately, it's still anybody's guess.

Bruce Mate's tagging of sperm whales also discovered, rather fascinatingly, that they twist upside down at the bottom of a deep dive. Why should they do such a curious thing? One suggestion is that this allows them to see the silhouette of a squid against the dim light of the surface. Maybe it allows them to see their teammates, too. Another theory is that, by twisting, they create a powerful suction effect that pulls the squid into their mouths from up to three feet away. So far, I'm sorry to say, no one knows.

The sperm whale's immense battles with the giant or colossal squid leave their marks. They are often seen with white scars on their bodies from squids' beaks, hooks and circular suction pads which suggest that the squid are not unconscious when a sperm whale grabs it.

Unfortunately no one has ever seen or filmed one of these battles but it would certainly make for intriguing viewing. However the sperm whales catch their squid I suspect it's very clever. After all, they have the largest brains of any animal in the world, maybe the universe – even larger than Stephen Hawking's. Whatever they do, they do it well. The Earth's population of sperm whales eat more marine life each year than humans do. Hopefully, we'll catch on to the sperm whale's secrets one day... and before the squid do. The quest goes on...

Before we finish with sperm whales it's worth noting that the 'stun' theory was presented (though not originally conjured) by Norris and Mohl in their research paper in 1983. They begin their article with the paragraph, *"In this paper we discuss an hypothesis. We marshall scattered supportive evidence, outline its problems, and explore its ramifications and suggest tests. We do not prove it."* More of a 'quality-irrelevant theory', then. *Good lads!*

Mirissa, as a small beach town, doesn't disappoint. It has a similar layout to Unawatuna presenting its beautiful banana-shaped beach with the roaring Indian Ocean relentlessly throwing wave after wave onto the shore. The restaurants and bars that line the sand are less developed, more rustic and more laid-back than Unawatuna. The food was good though, and the scenery couldn't be more idyllic.

In conducting further valuable research on the optimal methods for booking guesthouses I tried a new sophisticated technique of turning up and finding one. I hypothesised that a face to face negotiation, being there ready to take a room and being able to see it first, would give me stronger bargaining power.

As I trudged along Mirissa's quiet main country lane I stumbled into a youngish, friendly and alert tuk tuk driver who suggested a place just a stone's throw from the beach. The room was clean, spacious and had two double beds pushed together to form a quadruple bed! *Sold!!* The initial results of my research were favourable.

On my brief exploration I saw my first ever female tuk tuk driver drive past *(incredible!!)* and found a smart hotel called 'Club Mirissa' run by a friendly and helpful couple. Within minutes I was booked onto a whale watching tour for the next day at 4,000r (£20) and they let me use their internet.

Unhappily, Asha de Vos had not replied to my email. Trying not to feel downhearted I thought, *Sod it! I'll e-mail her again! If it's a Willie Thorne shot-to-nothing to email her once, it's a Willie Thorne shot-to-nothing to email her twice!*

Mirissa's beach is as close to paradise as I've ever seen. Relaxed bars and restaurants were dotted along the beach and the soft, warm sand flitted in and out of shade provided by a sprinkling of coconut trees. The best part, though, was the sea. The sea deepens sharply reaching the chest only a few metres out, then shallows again to the knee before finally sloping away on its journey to the Antarctic.

I was duty-bound to leave the tranquillity of the soft sand to attend my appointment of battle with The Indian Ocean. *I'm not one to shirk a challenge from anything as inconsequential as an entire ocean!* Our two great armies stood ready for conflict and The Indian Ocean took the initiative with a quick volley of waves. At first they came like jabs and I easily bounced over them. *You'll have to do better than that!* It did. A wave came along that, in close quarters, constituted a wall of water in front of me. It fed its power by sucking in the water from around me, the trickster, leaving me with less buoyancy to jump over it. I jumped up but was beaten backwards as the wave thumped into my chest. I just about managed to land on my feet, bent over facing backwards.

I decided to jump sideways on to make myself more streamlined and cut through the water. Another mighty wave came, bigger than the last one. I jumped up sideways on but didn't get high enough. The wave picked me up and slammed me back down from whence I came. It had stolen most of my water again and I landed on the seabed with only six inches of liquid to not soften the blow. Then the rest of the wave came crashing down on top of me and threw me around like a doll at the whim of the sea Gods. *I feel like I'm in a bloody washing machine!*

The big waves came in bundles; I picked myself up and jumped not high enough again. "I see I have under-estimated you, Sir". To upgrade my technique further I thought to jump up and forwards instead of straight up to maintain balance as the wave pushes me backwards.

My new sideways-on forward-jumping technique was clever enough to survive a bundle of monstrous waves the Indian Ocean threw at me. "I'm afraid, Sir, you don't have enough to defeat me!" I goaded.

Riled by my taunts the Indian Ocean mustered a more powerful effort still. I stood firm, staring up at a mountain of water advancing upon me. "Finally, a worthy challenge my keen adversary." Facing perfectly side on I jumped up and forward with magnificent splendour and was crushed completely. The mighty wave then picked me up in its clutches and smashed me against the seabed again before whirling me around some more. I was a passenger on the Indian Ocean express with my fate at the mercy of the Gods. Battered but not beaten I picked myself up for the onslaught to continue.

Battle raged on for centuries until, broken, exhausted and in utter defeat, I sloped off for a beer, lesson learned. The sea always wins.

On the 1st April 2012 I received an email from blue whale scientist, Asha de Vos!!

```
"Hi                                                   Gavin

Sorry for not getting back sooner but I am leaving
back                       to                  Australia
at the end of this week and so I am in Colombo. I have
a                       public                       talk
```

on the 5th in Colombo about the blue whales and you are welcome to attend if you are around. Shoot me an email.

Your adventures sound grand and I am sure you will have many wonderful experiences around our coastlines. If you are in the city this week get in touch and we can talk.....not sure how else to do it since I am not around in the south at the moment?

Hope all is well and good luck finding the giants of the ocean!
Asha

```
     --
><((((°>`·.¸¸.·´¯`·.¸.·´¯`·....¸><((((°>¸.·
`·.¸¸.·´¯`·.¸¸.·´¯`·..
><((((°>`·.¸¸.·´¯`·.¸.·´¯`·....¸><((((°>"
```

Hah! With a change of vague plan-like expectation I gave my old friend Dammika a call for a re-visit to Colombo.

The following day I saw blue whales... at least 15 of the blighters!! *They're as common as muck around here.*

The day started by meeting at Club Mirissa for breakfast and sea sickness tablets at 7:00am. There I met a Canadian called Ryan and a pleasant German couple, Michi and Oliver, who were accompanying me on the ~~hunt~~ search for blue whales. I briefly explained to them the rules and beauty of cricket before we were whisked off to the harbour (these unfortunate Germans didn't even know what a 'run' was. *Good grief!).*

Our boat was perhaps 50ft long and could carry some 25 passengers more than the 12 on board. I couldn't understand why it wasn't near full – we were off to see blue whales!!

In accordance with their policy we were all issued with life jackets which, as is my policy, I casually threw on the empty bench. No one was in anyway bothered. Cumbersome things, they just get in the way and I had every intention of staying in the boat and faith in my own ability to accomplish that.

With so few people on board there was plenty of space and we were free to wander about as we pleased. Some people began to feel seasick and I pondered why those land-lovers stayed upstairs where the boat's sway was amplified. As the boat cruised along flying fish darted out of the water and glided a foot or two above the surface for 50 metres or so. *Why do they bother doing that?* I thought. Apparently it's to evade predators.

"WHALE!!" a crew member yelled on spying the tall blow of a blue whale. *There she blows!* Blue whales are known for having spectacularly tall, vertical, single-column blows when they come up to breathe – about as high as a house (a sperm whale's blowhole is at the front and left of their head and they blow at a 45° angle). Another sign to look for to identify a whale is the dorsal fin which, on blues, is unusually small.

The boat's engines fired up and we motored towards the whale. Everyone scampered to find a good spot to see the whale as the top of its head broke the surface. Its back and the bulk of its tail then followed before it sank back below. This solitary whale cruised along the surface, bobbing up and down to take a few breaths.

The size of this creature was immense and it swam at a surprising 30mph or more. It is difficult to appreciate just how big they are from pictures but here, even from quite far away, it was breath-taking. Blue whales are shy creatures, much more shy than the attention-adoring and flamboyant humpback whales, so Stephen Fry purports in that whale documentary. Perhaps blue whales have longer memories and can still recall their brethren showing too much interest in boats and meeting harpoons. Or perhaps the blue whales that remain from those dark days are all the ones that are naturally shy and cautious and avoided the hunting ships. They may then pass their cautious outlook on life to their offspring, either genetically or through parental guidance.

This, the first blue whale I ever saw, was just as shy as the reports say. After a few minutes he bobbed up for the last time and heaved even more of its great bulk out of the water and arched its back. "TAIL, TAIL!!" shouted a crewman. The whale's entire fluke proudly emerged from the water, erect and glorious before slowly sinking back down into the abyss. This whale was probably beginning a deep dive to feed and will likely be down there for 10 minutes or so.

We stood at the side of the boat looking for the tell-tale sign of the blue whale's tall vertical blow. It wasn't often long between whale sightings. Each sighting followed the same pattern as the first. It would cruise along for a while, bob up and down and spring its fluke out of the water to mark the start of its dive and would disappear into the deep blue. The blue whales showed their fluke almost every time they dived – it was the highlight of the sighting. Surprisingly often we saw two blue whales cruising together, a mother and her smaller calf. Sometimes, they poked their heads out of the water too, maybe having a look to see what was around.

They will have seen four other boats like ours all looking for, and finding, blue whales. One boat was in particularly bad repair. Its engine could be heard over our own and black smoke billowed from its rear. In contrast, our boat seemed reasonably responsible. Whenever a whale was spotted the captain would motor over towards it but keep a healthy distance. We didn't approach a whale from directly behind but, if possible, would run a course in parallel so that the whale swam in front and to the left or right of us. This, apparently, is responsible whale watching conduct.

That said I still got the impression that our captain and crew didn't really know much about these whales. A ten minute talk from Asha de Vos would be full of information completely new to them. From reading this book you already know more about blue whales than they did.

The whale, poking his head out of the water, may have also seen the monstrous container ships rounding the southern tip of Sri Lanka on their way to various parts of the world. Here lies one of the busiest shipping lanes in the world.

There was forever a dirty great container ship on the horizon going about its business. I quite like them. I still find it amazing how all that metal can float and it's an exciting idea to have these small towns that float around the globe.

They're no good for the whales though. On 20th March 2012, one of these enormous ships rolled into Colombo's port completely unaware that a dead blue whale lay draped over its bulbous bow. It seems these whales and the container ships operate, alarmingly, in the same waters.

I wondered how far from shore the whales lived so looked towards land and found I could still see land on the horizon. *Horizon!?*

Aha, maybe my horizon formula can make another appearance. I could see the cliffs and trees but not the beach; a stroke of luck that the point where the sea met the land must have been ever-so-slightly beyond the horizon. Standing on the boat I was maybe 6 or 7 metres above sea level which I roughly estimated meant we were between 8km and 11km out. *In the context of blue whales, that doesn't sound far at all.*

Seeing the blue whale was a magical experience. I would recommend it to anyone but try to use a responsible whale watching company. This would not only help make whale watching businesses realise that this is important to customers but provides a more fulfilling experience. Sometimes I felt anxious that our boat would misbehave. I would have felt awful if we had disturbed the whales to the point of discomfort. It was a shame I didn't see any sperm whales or dolphins. Apparently, blue whales and sperm whales don't mix.

Back in Mirissa I bumped into Copper Steve and Dave again. They had come here straight after the cricket to enjoy the beach, see the whales and be defeated in battle by the Indian Ocean. Steve and Dave had been whale watching the day before and saw thirty sperm whales and two blue whales. *This has got to be one of the best whale watching places in the world.* Regrettably, however, they also saw a dead and mutilated blue whale floating in the water. They suspected it had tangled with one of those container ships and its propeller. It seems the container ships present a very real and regular danger.

We sat in a bar on the beach watching the first day of the second cricket test in Colombo on the telly between power cuts. At lunch, as Steve and Dave primed themselves to dual with the Ocean once more, it was time for me to leave Mirissa and see about finding this blue whale scientist.

Chapter 15 – Colombo (Part 2)

I happily paid almost nothing for a bus to hurtle me to Colombo grabbing lunch and some child's maths homework on the way.

In need of a shower, food and perhaps a little drink I arrived at Dammika's and was welcomed back with gleeful enthusiasm. "GAVIN!!! I have a bottle for you. You go, have a shower and then we'll have a drink." *Dammika is a legend.*

Before I could take two steps towards the shower an enormous, sixty year old Englishman with thinning white hair and a craving for attention introduced himself and a kilo of fillet steak that he'd so proudly bought for only £3 and described in every detail for twenty minutes.

This was Fat Derek. He very quickly presented himself as a pompous, opinionated know-it- all who liked to prattle away for hours in a one-way conversation conveying that he knew everything there was to know about everything. He must have sensed after a while that I doubted his 'facts' so reluctantly ended sections of monologue with "or so I believe anyway" or "well that's what I think".

Then he would move swiftly on to something else like the quality (or lack of quality) of Sri Lanka's water - much to Dammika's disagreement, or the state (undeveloped state) of Sri Lanka's tourism industry and how Dammika should get some kind of automated lock on his front gate so he doesn't have to wait up for people.

Derek had worked as an engineer on trucks for twenty years before owning and running a camping and caravan park in Wales for another twenty years. As such he enjoyed giving Dammika (who he called Dammy) advice about the "hospitality game".

Together we drank Old Arrack on Dammika's porch and eventually paid our collective attention to my two apparent travelling quandaries:

1. I wanted to spend time in the highly recommended, beautiful southern hill country highlights of Ella, Nuwara Eliya (little England), World's End and Adam's Peak but this detour to Colombo had thrown me off kilter.
2. Dammika pointed out that my plan to fly to Thailand on 14th or 15th April hit a snag as the 12th – 15th was a Sri Lankan holiday for the Buddhist New Year and everything from buses to guesthouses, tuk tuks and shops shuts down. It sounded like no place for a traveller.

Three drunken heads are better than one, we supposed, and the solutions came to pass as follows:

1. I get an early train the day after Asha de Vos' lecture to the far end of the hill county – Ella. It will take most of the day but then I can spend a week slowly working my way through the hill country back to Colombo.
2. Although Dammika offered a room at his home, even though he was closed and out of the city, I opted to leave Sri Lanka before the whole place shuts down. I will fly to Bangkok just before the New Year celebrations on the 12th April.

Derek went to bed at 9pm, apparently later than usual.

I spent much of the following day with Fat Derek. He had come to Sri Lanka to watch the cricket and, like myself, had found Dammika Home to be the cheapest guesthouse in Colombo. As I sat down to watch the cricket on TV I saw, on Dammika's coffee table, a book by Oliver Sacks - 'The man who mistook his wife for a hat'. *I recognise that book – aha, it's the same book my friend gave me. Ahh, it's my book!! What a stroke of good fortune.*

Derek and I were casually watching the morning session (10am – 12pm) when I remembered, in Galle, they opened the gates at tea so people can watch the evening session for free. "I reckon I'll go to the game at tea and watch the evening session before this whale lecture", I told Derek.
"If you do, I'll come with you, if that's alright?" he said, and it was.

As we made our way to the ground I learned Derek's rather appealing story. His caravan park was doing OK until, as Derek put it, he "fucked up" by investing a huge amount of money in improvements, expansions and modernisations that were never going to generate the income to justify them. *That's refreshingly honest, Fat Derek.* To compound matters the government, shortly after, warned the entire country that if they go to the countryside they will catch foot and mouth disease. As such Derek was left with a mountain of debt and splendid new facilities that no one came to. This inevitably meant that Derek's caravan park soon became the bank's caravan park.

He was broke, but not bankrupt. He ensured that all of his debts were paid and found himself a farmer's shack to rent for a paltry rent. He stayed there for a few years, getting by… just. Eventually, the farmer required his shack again leaving Derek in some strife to find somewhere affordable to live. With a severe bout of generosity Derek's Dad bought a house for Derek to live in but, sadly, died soon after.

Derek reflected how a person's confidence and self-esteem can take a serious dip in form by not having a job or a business... a purpose I suppose, and the ability to provide for yourself. It has an enormous impact on a person's happiness and wellbeing.

Furthermore, throughout these low years Derek had been diagnosed with cancer, defeated it, and then suffered a heart attack. He says, "Having effectively died twice, I now have a different perception of time."

Derek doesn't have much money, or much youth, but he has a rare honesty and humility about his mistakes and flaws. He puts an emphasis on what you can do with *time,* instead of *money* and maintains an optimistic disposition. Anyone who can go to Sri Lanka to watch Test cricket AND buy a kilo of fillet steak for £3 hasn't got much to moan about, I'm sure Derek would agree.

I took a seat in the middle of the city bus and Derek took two. The bus soon filled up, and when Sri Lankan buses fill up everyone gets to know each other intimately. They squeezed themselves together and stuffed themselves into any and every space available. In getting on and off it seems accepted behaviour to forcefully shove fellow passengers aside as necessary to get through – what else can be done?

"Let's get off here, Derek", I shouted across the crowded aisle. "This is about right." With the girth of several Sri Lankan men Fat Derek was not the usual prospect the locals contended with on these buses. I fought my way to the door whilst laughing uncontrollably at watching Fat Derek squeeze himself past a dozen or so deeply unfortunate people. "Sorry! I'm very sorry", he bellowed as he crushed fellow passengers with his massive belly. Only God knows how he managed it.

At the cricket ground the final session had just begun. Instead of open gates we found a particularly unhelpful young official charging us 6,000r (£30) for a ticket. "At tea!?" I exclaimed.
"6,000 rupees", he repeated. *I'm not going to pay that for less than two hours' cricket, and there's no way Derek is.*

"Let's have a walk round the ground, Derek, and see if these gates are open further round." He agreed and as we walked lots of different tuk tuk drivers tried to sell us tickets. Not wanting to waste time Derek managed to negotiate tickets for us both for 1,000r (£5). The tuk tuk driver whisked us round the corner to an open gate for people to enter freely and demanded his 1,000r. We both immediately had this fella down as a scally wag running a scam, but, with the honour of a gentleman, Derek handed over his 500r as he'd agreed. I was feeling less honourable but before I could decide whether to relent to this scoundrel or not a nearby policeman had him down as a scally wag running a scam and promptly removed him.

Surrounded by jubilant and friendly Sri Lankan supporters Derek and I sat back with a couple of beers and watched Kevin Pietersen, in generous spirits, give us two sixes, give England 151 runs and give Sri Lanka his wicket with ANOTHER silly sweep shot!

After leaving Derek at the cricket to see Ash de Vos' lecture I only saw him once more. At about 9:00pm that night I had almost made it back to the guesthouse when I bumped into Dammika on Galle Road looking a tad flustered. "Ahh Gavin", he said "how was your day?"
"Oh, very good, thanks. I'm afraid England won the cricket" I said.
"Yes, I saw. Where is… err… ", Dammika looked forgetful, then held his arms out to the side "…… the fat guy!?"
"What!? He's not home?" I asked with astonishment.
"No. I thought he'd be back by now. He doesn't know Colombo very well." I knew how easy it could be to get lost in an unknown city and felt a pang of concern.

We walked back to Dammika's house and opened another bottle of Old Arrack. The evening reached 10pm before a sweaty and grubby Fat Derek staggered onto Dammika's front porch terrifically past his bed time. He'd been walking the streets of Sri Lanka's capital for hours not knowing which bus to catch nor mustering the financial frivolity to pay for a tuk tuk. He could barely summon the energy to talk about it and, with a heave-ho up the porch step, went straight to bed. I never saw Fat Derek again.

By that time I considered Fat Derek to be a smashing bloke of a rare, honourable breed. His know-it-all first impression, I later concluded, was probably his exceptional effort to be sociable and likable. Maybe he was trying a little too hard, I don't know, but after getting to know him better I realised he's got huge heart that I hope doesn't fail him again.

I arrived early to the Lakshman Kadirgamar Institute in central Colombo. It wasn't far from the cricket ground and my tuk tuk driver was a committed one. The lady on the desk couldn't seem to find my name on her list but she let me in anyway. *Jolly decent of her.*

"Hello, please come in", a sweet voice encouraged as I poked my head through the large wooden doors of the lecture theatre. Asha de Vos smiled a beautiful smile at me as she stood at the front of the nearly empty room and welcomed me in. "Hi, I'm Gavin Anderson. I've been emailing you about meeting to talk… er…"

"Ah yes, Gavin, I'm glad you could make it. Did you find the whales?"

We talked for a little while about the blue whales off Mirissa and my trip to Sri Lanka. Asha is a young, attractive woman with a joyful, pretty face. She has a contagious smile and a disposition that looked for reasons to laugh. Behind that happy-go-lucky demeanour you could see a passion, a strength and an intelligence that the blue whales bring to the fore.

"Do you scuba dive?" she asked.

"I love scuba diving," I replied "and hope to do some on this trip at some point."

"There is some excellent diving from Colombo. If you get chance you should do it. I went this morning, I love it too. I don't really have the time for it, I have to fly back to Australia tomorrow and I have to get everything ready and see my parents, but I couldn't resist", she confessed. "I love it so much", Asha continued, "my mother says if I'm not on the water I'm in the water."

"Ha, perhaps you were a fish in a former life…" I japed. *Hang on, this girl is all about whales…* "…or a WHALE!" I corrected. An awkward expression flashed across Asha's face. It was there for only a fraction of a second but I'll never forget it. It was a blend of surprise, confusion and disgust. *Oh dear! She thinks I've called her a whale! And… I did, but not like…*

"Well, blue whales are actually quite streamlined", she smiled with generosity and grace as she stroked the sides of her body, "so I'll take that as a compliment."

"Yes, and so you should but, I didn't mean it like that." I laughed off. *Oh, it's no use.* "Anyway, it's been lovely talking to you. Good luck with the lecture." *Good God, Gavin,* I chastised myself as Asha greeted other attendees and the lecture theatre began to fill up.

I had no idea what to expect but, by now, I had stopped expecting anything. Each place and each day was so different and unknown that expectations didn't really serve a purpose anymore. I took my seat and noticed the crisp smartness of the lecture theatre and everyone in it, Asha's fellow academics, students, journalists, scientists, professors and other distinguished ladies and gentlemen in the world of whales. I was there on a jolly wearing a crumpled shirt, shorts and flip flops, slightly inebriated and fresh from watching the cricket with Fat Derek. If that's not enough I seem to have accidentally offended the lecturer before she's even begun! *No, I'm sure she's too thick skinned for that – oh no, there I go again. Broad shoulders?*

Not a moment too soon the lecture began. Asha explained that these "unorthodox" whales are the only known "resident population" of whales in the world and went on to describe her research, but these stubborn blue whales, for the most part, still retained their mysticism.

Asha and her colleagues still have little idea about whale communication and interpreting their sounds; not many people can make any strides forward with that. Asha talked about how blue whales around the world ordinarily show their flukes on around 20% of their dives but the blue whales close to Sri Lanka show theirs on 85% of dives observed. Why should that be? Perhaps they are making steeper dives? No one knows.

Asha also mentioned that the whale population lived about 10km out to sea which, I was pleased to note, was consistent with my earlier estimations using my horizon formula.

The bulk of Asha's lecture was about the dangers the whales face from human activity. The newly-opened waters and the discovery of the whales created a surge in whale watching. Unfortunately the authorities haven't caught on nearly as quickly and there was no whale watching regulation in place. Regulation is in force in the most popular whale watching countries like Canada, Australia and Iceland detailing how close boats are allowed to get, how many boats can gather around one whale, how to follow a whale and that sort of thing. Asha de Vos is concerned that over-pestering whales will cause them to leave the area and would like to see regulations come in as soon as possible. It seems to me that 'pestering' is about as much damage as whale watching boats can cause, and everyone gets pestered most every day. I'm not sure I would call it 'dangerous'.

What is dangerous to the whales is having that hectically busy shipping lane on their doorstep. Asha made reference to the blue whale found draped over the bulbous bow of the container ship as it pulled into Colombo Port. She also produced a photo of a blue whale fatally wounded, she says, by a ship's propeller just a couple of days previous. *Hang on, that'll be the dead whale Copper Steve saw on his trip.* (Furthermore, The New York Times ran the story on 3rd July 12 about this same dead whale to highlight the threat shipping traffic poses to the blue whales.)

At the time of the lecture in early April 2012 six blue whales had been found killed by container ships in Sri Lankan waters since the turn of the year but who knows how many more killed whales remain undiscovered. A whale getting hit by a gigantic ship is a worldwide occurrence but it seems all too common in Sri Lanka where so many blue whales share the same waters with such a busy shipping lane.

Asha de Vos is pushing for the shipping lane to be moved further out so that the whales are much less likely to encounter them. A great idea for the whales but the ships, having to travel further, would incur more costs in fuel, wages, maintenance and such like. I wish her well but Asha is likely to face fierce opposition from the shipping companies and I fear that she would have more success doing battle with the Indian Ocean on Mirissa Beach.

I later found that the whale watching boats may be exacerbating the problem after all. The New York Times article included a keen insight into the problem by none other than Asha de Vos. Although she didn't mention it in the lecture Asha is quoted suggesting that the whale watching boats could be driving the whales further out to sea and into the container ship infested waters of the shipping lanes. The article then moves on to describe Asha's uphill struggle with the authorities in trying to provide protection for the whales.

During the question and answer session at the end of the lecture one fella asks a particularly poignant question. "Why don't the whales avoid the container ships?" As ever with blue whales it is a mystery and one to my mind that Asha and her colleagues should like to look into. Asha described a theory they currently have which is that ships make noise at a similar frequency to the one whales use and they can't make it out. That sounds wholly unsatisfactory to my ears.

I did find, however, an article in the Independent that offers "The Lloyd Mirror Effect" (???). "The Lloyd Mirror Effect" is an acoustic shadow in front of a large ship that results from the engines being at the stern and the sound of them blocked by the rest of the ship. As a result, a whale in the path of an approaching ship is unlikely to hear it.

It makes sense, then, for the ship to have some kind of whale alarm to tell the whale to stay away but the Independent conveniently looked into that too. "Studies of ship alarms have shown that whales react in a way that actually would increase the chances of getting struck." Curiosity killed the blue whale, perhaps. Surely, though, there is a sound in blue whale language which means 'Back of, Pal! I'm rather large and unpleasant.' So we know that we don't know what that sound is - it would be an exciting research project to find out.

I wondered if most collisions might happen when the whales are sleeping. They don't usually drop into a deep sleep like we do because, being voluntary breathers, they need to remember to breathe. Instead they shut down half their brain and have what is thought to be something similar to a nap whilst floating on the surface. I would wager a half-asleep whale is less likely to notice a one hundred thousand ton container ship than a waked one. Perhaps it might like an alarm to inform it of the ship's approach.

I left the lecture and considered how to get back to Dammika's. The unfamiliar streets of a large, alien Colombo felt haunting and mysterious in the dark. I walked west thinking that I'd soon meet Galle Road where a bus will almost stop for me and hotfoot me south to Dammika Home.

On my adventurous walk towards Galle Road was a futuristic stadium or arena that was buzzing with people, soldiers and their guns. The exotic looking structure is set back from the road some 100 yards by a huge car park. The customers, if that's what they were, drifted their way towards this grand and flamboyant arena dressed smartly and behaving impeccably. A serious looking young soldier, rifle in arms, softened his expression when he saw me walking towards him.

"Hello", he said.
"Hello", I mirrored. "What is this place?" With broken English he managed to convey that it was the National Theatre. *Ah, splendid.* "It's very impressive", I said and he smiled and waggled his head in agreement. Figuring that that was the most information I was likely to get from this chap I continued my course towards Galle Road.

Buying a drink, as I did then, revealed a most peculiar consistent inconsistency. A 500ml bottle of Coca Cola costs 85r (43p) whilst a 330ml can of Coca Cola costs 120r (60p). This was the case in every coke-selling shop I had set foot in whilst in Sri Lanka, from little stores run by a solitary old man to the large supermarkets. Why is it that a smaller can costs more than a larger bottle? I bought a bottle (obviously) and felt the desperate need for some form of meat.

Meat is a rare delight in Sri Lanka. Most meals contain only a scrap of meat if any at all and tonight my body craved it. I popped into another little shop and found that I could buy half a rubbish chicken for 400r (£2). It was a scrawny, dry looking carcass and wholly unsatisfactory. The next shop selling chicken made the same appalling offer. It seems, in Sri Lanka, it is easier to buy opium than it is a plump piece of chicken. And also, how is it that it costs more for half a scrawny chicken than it does in England for half a decent chicken? *Surely, with low costs for land and wages, they should be able to produce decent chickens for less than this. What the hell is going on?*

I'd be tempted to start a chicken farm out in the hill country, breed hundreds of decent chickens and sell them to these shops so the hardworking, near-honest people of Colombo could have some chunky, juicy chickens to eat. If you happen to know a thing or two about chicken farming I'd warrant you could make a very nice home for yourself in Sri Lanka.

I should think that with a new chicken farming industry, as well as the development of world-class whale watching and a space rocket launch programme, Sri Lanka's economy could be boosted immeasurably over the coming years (should you be reading, Mr President... or The Admiral).

My meat craving forced me, reluctantly, into MacDonalds. I am constantly impressed that any MacDonalds restaurant you care to visit, anywhere in the world, will serve you food to the *precise* same abominable specification as any other. Even in the most far flung corners of the Earth they are unwaveringly determined that not an ounce of real quality should accidentally leak into their products. In an ever-changing world with vast differences in climate, cultures and economies there is always, at least, that consistency. It leaves me confounded and impressed in equal measures that they lure me into their restaurants about twice a year.

After gobbling down a cluster of Chicken Mcnuggets, I must shamefully admit, I felt satisfied and it provided a welcome change from rice and curry. *I wonder where they get their chicken from.* Actually, I won't look into that. At least they had proper wash basins and not those awful McWash's that insist on giving you soap, water and hot air when *it* wants to and not when you want it to (silly idea).

I eventually arrived at Dammika's and prepared for my day's train journey to Ella. "Dammika, I've been meaning to ask you something for a while", I remembered.
"Oh yes, Gavin. I hope I can answer it for you", he replied, helpfully.
"Well, I keep seeing people spit red stuff on the floor. Why do they do that?" I asked.
"It is a habit", he didn't explain.
"Yes, but... why?"
It turns out this habit is maintained mostly by Tamil people. From what information I could glean from Dammika they get a beetle leaf, a nut type thing, something involving lime (which gives the red colour, peculiarly) and tobacco. Everything is folded into the leaf and chewed for a while. His garbled explanation was slightly unsatisfactory in details so I have researched it.

What they actually have is a betel leaf, an areca nut, slaked lime and, depending on taste, tobacco all wrapped up to make a 'quid' – a little parcel. Wikipedia describes a quid as "an addictive psycho-stimulating and euphoria-inducing formulation with adverse health effects". It made me wonder about the bus drivers chewing this stuff but apparently it heightens alertness. It is comparable to a cup of coffee… although people don't tend to spit their coffee onto the pavement.

The stimulating properties come from both the betel leaf and the areca nut, which isn't a nut but a fruit. These two things are the epitomes of partners having been close friends for at least 4,000 years (according to archaeological evidence). Many Asian cultures refer to them in wedding ceremonies inspiring many young couples to live together as well as the betel leaf and areca nut. Lennon and McCartney, Batman and Robin, Nelson and Hardy, Beardsley and Lineker, the Chuckle brothers, Bert and Ernie, and even the brothers Bee Gee are no partnerships as strong as these two. The adverse health effects mentioned refers to evidence that they dramatically increase the risk of cancer, particularly in the mouth.

In time they were joined by slaked lime (which is Calcium Hydroxide) used in making roads, hair removal creams, break discs, mortar for dentistry, corn tortillas, pickling vegetables and helping digestion when folded up inside betel leaves.

Chapter 16 – The Trains

To decline a prostitute is a unique type of business refusal. I am yet to find a way of doing it that doesn't hurt the poor prostitute's feelings. "No thanks", "I'm not interested", "I don't sleep with prostitutes", "That's too expensive" all equate to "I don't fancy you enough" – enough to either part with current moral protocol or the required cash. At 5am, at a bus stop on Galle Road, I was reacquainted with this quandary.

"Hey mister, you wanna good time?" I turned to see a muscular individual wearing liberally and, I'd wager, drunkenly applied make-up strut towards me, grinning. I rubbed my blurry eyes and tried to shake myself awake a little. "You wanna have some fun?" he or she (???) enquired again. *No I do not!* "You should come with me", she enticed further, "and we can play together". I gestured to the bus stop. "No thanks love. I've got to catch a bus", I explained, considering this plainly obvious.

"You don't like me?" she sulked. *Oh no!* This represents the worst possible outcome for an English gentleman. "How could anyone possibly not like you?" I clumsily blurted out. *Oh God, I've made it worse.* "I don't even know you, to be fair; it's just that I must get this bus. I'm sure you're delightful and... and beautiful of course", LIAR, GAVIN! YOU'RE A LIAR!! "This is really an inconvenient time. I've just got up, you know". *Where IS this bus, for heaven's sake!*

"So you have a room near here?" she whispered attempting allure. It is quite extraordinary how tricky some people make it to not hurt their feelings. "No, no room. Only a bus to catch", and like a gleaming white knight one of those marvellous buses rescued me from this prickly predicament and veritably flew me down an empty Galle Road to Fort Station.

The morning had not even reached 6am when I suffered a second hullaballoo of the day. I presented myself at the ticket counter fifteen minutes in advance to buy a 1st class ticket that, it transpired, must be bought at least fourteen days in advance. *Blast!*

The animated ticket cashier flustered and shouted in Sinhalese to people behind him and presented me to an unknown gentleman who whisked me off to the front carriage of the train. The grandmother of a Sri Lankan family had felt too unwell to travel with her 1st class ticket and the remaining 17 members of the family were, therefore, on the look-out for a confused moron who had turned up without one. By some happy fortune, that was me.

They treated me like one of the family making sure I was fed and watered from their travel-stores of fruit, sandwiches and snacks. The man next to me was friendly and healthy, carrying a bit more flesh on his bones than the average Sri Lankan bloke. He was an accountant by trade and led his family with a blend of warmth and discipline.

We talked for much of the journey about cricket, the hill-country, whether I had a girlfriend, Sri Lankan businesses and their energy infrastructure. He was a knowledgeable bloke. He told me that about 80% of Sri Lanka's power supply comes from oil and the remaining 20% from clean hydroelectric, but that can be as much as 35% in the wet season (the UK's clean fuel consumption is only 9.2%).

This educated and successful gent surprised me further. "What made you come to Sri Lanka? Was it the cricket?" he asked me.
"I did see the cricket but I came here to see the blue whales", I replied.
"The what?"
"The blue whales. There are lots of them just off the south coast", I explained.
"You travelled all this way just to see these… blue whales?" he asked with the disbelieving shock of meeting the most stupid man on the planet. I couldn't understand his bafflement.
"Yes, of course. I think it could be one of the best whale watching sites in the world. The blue whale is the largest animal to have ever lived on the planet, you know."
"What!?" he exclaimed, "really… bigger than an elephant!?" *Oh, right. I see.*

How can it be that this educated Sri Lankan gent doesn't know what a blue whale is, and there are so many so close? Have I incorrectly assumed for all these years that everyone is fascinated by blue whales? Maybe they're not… Maybe it's just me???

One of the great things about these trains (aside from a 9 hour journey in 1st class costing 640r (£3.20)) is that you can open the large, wooden-framed windows stationed at each seat and stick your head out. It was an invigorating feeling to have the cool wind rush round my face and through my hair, but mainly it was a joy that they let you do it. You can't do that kind of thing in Britain, not even on the buses.

Which is more, you can open the door and stick your whole body out of it whilst holding tightly to the hand rail for dear life. This was my favourite pass-time on the train, especially through the jungle terrain of the hill country where long tunnels and dramatic, expansive views were plentiful. Hanging out of the train door as it clings to the mountain side is a thrilling feeling that I can highly recommend if you have a strong grip.

The train guard sat in his office at the end of our carriage and his complete disinterest in me, and everyone else draping themselves out of the door, indicated that this was an accepted activity. I'm quite sure they'd let you climb on the roof, do cartwheels and kill yourself if you so wished...and why not in a free country?

A thunderous downpour came to cut through the heat of the day. The windows came down and were lashed by the heavy rain creating a loud growling rumble through the carriage. The bright sunshine had made way for a gloominess that had become unfamiliar. Maybe it was age, having spent all my years in Britain growing too accustomed to the rain, but it was a welcome sight to me. I remained at my open doorway until I was wet and cold and loved every second of it. There is life in the rain, I think.

The train, however, had no love for the rain. Our incline in the wet conditions allowed the train to make no progress at all. The crew threw sand on the track and achieved a speed marginally quicker than 'stop'. We made a little more than no progress in over an hour or two giving one of the chattier brothers in my adopted family time to tell me about Bhutan.

I had ignorantly never heard of Bhutan so I didn't know what he was talking about until he began right at the start. Bhutan is a landlocked country, half the size of Sri Lanka, wedged between India and China with Nepal to its west and Bangladesh to its south. My new friend told me I should visit but a visa would cost me a rather unfriendly $200 a day. He had been there at the invitation of the Royal Family who needed his expert help with their IT systems – as is his job.

Bhutan has a population below a million but is a thriving economy thanks chiefly to its new Tala Hydroelectric Project that opened in 2008 and takes advantage of Bhutan's mountainous terrain to produce clean electricity from falling water (Hydroelectric power now accounts for 16% of the world's electricity consumption). Bhutan's gigantic Tala Hydroelectric Project produces 4,865 GWh/yr and sells the jolly lot to India.

This scenic train journey was taking me to Ella, the east-most end of the hill-country. With seven days before my flight from Colombo I could enjoy a couple of days in Ella before moving on to World's End, Nuwara Eliya (Little England) and Adam's Peak.

World's End, found at Horton Plains, is so named because the landscape suddenly ends with a dramatic 870 metre sheer drop not unlike, so they say, the end of the world. To see the views one must get there excruciatingly early in the morning before the mist descends. Even so, when the mist does conceal the valley below it is said you really feel like you're at the end of the world. This is one of Sri Lanka's main attractions I was keen to see.

The other must-see spectacle of the hill country is Adam's Peak, a conical mountain 2,243 metres high that Sri Lankans revere most highly. Near the top is a 1.8 metre rock formation in the shape of a footprint said to belong to Adam, Buddha, Shiva or St Thomas, depending on what religion you follow, made when he landed from the heavens. The proposition that God chose Sri Lanka to be Adam's landing destination on Earth has apparently gained further momentum by the recent discovery that Sri Lanka has the lowest gravitational force on the planet making God's task of delivering Adam 0.015% easier.

Visitors are encouraged to get up at 2am and climb Adam's Peak in the dark to see the sun rise from around 5:30am. A temple sits atop Sri Lanka's 'holy mountain' accessed by a number of lighted and stepped pathways. Every Sri Lankan Buddhist aims to see the sun rise from Adam's Peak at least once in their life-time.

My adopted family for the day eventually reached their stop and left me to hang out the door on the way to Ella. I must say, the train is a fine way to travel in Sri Lanka.

Chapter 17 – Ella

Why did the chicken cross the road? …… Because it can! In fact, it can go wherever it likes. In Ella, and most of rural Asia, chickens are seen wandering around, free as birds, all over the place. I don't know who owns them or how they keep track of them but it's a common practice in lots of different countries and with lots of different animals. Whilst in the Peruvian jungle in 2010 I met an incredible woman living in a hut in the jungle. Running freely around her grounds was a sheep, some dogs, cats, kittens, ducks, hens, chickens, new born chicks, fat guinea pigs and a turkey of which none were tied up or caged. Even so they remained in and around the hut blissfully unaware that they could be picked up, cooked and eaten imminently, as happened when I was present to one unlucky guinea pig.

The main mountain road finds a sleepy Ella and, almost as quickly, leaves her behind. Ella is a small, quiet, jungle village that has only recently acquired electricity and can be explored thoroughly in fifteen minutes. The occasional dirt track juts off the main road leading to a few more animals casually roaming around affordable, good quality guesthouses. A sprinkling of restaurants well caters for ravenous travellers fresh from sampling the region's excellent walking and cycling opportunities. Set high in the hill-country Ella enjoys green and fresh views of the mountainous jungle and tea plantations. It's fair to say I liked this place immediately.

Ella provided a welcome coolness after the blistering heat of the previous three weeks. It was an enjoyable return to my conventional practices to shower with hot water, and the first time I had wanted to.

My guesthouse was a three-storey, free standing building with the family-owner's residence on the ground floor and four comfortable rooms on each floor above that. There was a communal open-air eating area on the first floor where guests could relax and enjoy the views in the cool breeze.

Five minutes' walk away I found the most delicious best chicken khottu (perhaps that's why the chicken crossed the road). A chicken khottu, should you be wondering, is a straightforward traditional Sri Lankan dish that involves a chef throwing noodles, unspecified vegetables and chicken on a hot plate, with a few spices, and speedily chops the lot into pieces with two cleavers as it cooks. To hear the distant heavy rattle of cleavers on hot plate is a boost to the spirits for such a sound means there must be chicken khottu available nearby.

At breakfast I met a middle-aged Australian couple who were touring Sri Lanka. "I've come here to see the blue whales", I explained. "You can see blue whales here?" one of them asked with surprise. I explained about the unorthodox nature of these blue whales and that I'd seen a whole bunch of them. "Oh, we love whale watching", the Ozzy woman said. "We saw humpback whales off the coast of Australia. They are funny creatures – show offs."

Once again I was bemused that people were unaware of the magnificent whale watching that could be had from Mirissa but, in this case, heartened that they displayed some enthusiasm for it.

Towards the end of breakfast along came a slightly younger Dutch couple and a very similar conversation developed with them. Both couples, as experienced adventurers, maintained a flexible approach to their travel plans and immediately arranged to share a taxi to Mirissa the following morning. In return for the blue whale tip-off, and knowing I had just arrived in Ella, they told me about a short walk through tea plantations to a place known as 'Little Adam's Peak' and the more challenging adventure to Ella Rock.

The naming of 'Little Adam's Peak' appears to be conjured by some fiendishly cunning and soulless marketing folk. Little Adam's Peak bears no obvious resemblance to Adam's Peak at all ignoring obvious differences in scale. It is not the same shape of peak, there is no temple or Adam's footprint at the top and no widespread aspirations to climb it. Putting that ignorable indiscretion to one side it provided a convenient introductory two-hour walk.

This mini-adventure involved mostly flat and manageable terrain, fields of tea, constant views and a fella selling jewellery that he made from the white and black seeds of the tree he was presently sat beneath. His necklaces, bracelets and such were appealing enough but I found it difficult to believe all the intriguing photos and postcards sent to him from people all over the world thanking this chap for selling them a seed necklace. I kept to my usual disposition and bought precisely nothing.

Upon my arrival at the top of Little Adam's Peak I was hit by the captivating views over the deep valley. I sat on a small stone slab on the top for some rest, water and biscuits and drank in the scenery. As I looked left the vast Sri Lankan landscape stretched for miles in glorious, mountainous greenery. Straight across, and much higher up, stood Ella

Rock – a climb more adventurous than I imagined, and partway up was the impressive Rawana waterfalls – a local tourist attraction it was said was worth seeing.

By the time I returned to my guesthouse, after another satisfying chicken khottu, the Australian and Dutch couples were relaxing with cold beers. During their day's activities they had met an America couple and dutifully notified them of the magnificent whale watching to be had in Mirissa. These Americans, in turn, immediately altered their plans to see the blue whales too. *This is more like it!*

That afternoon I met a delightful Danish family staying at my guesthouse, the father of which was Karsten, a friendly chap, intelligent and fun. They seemed like the perfectly imperfect family with all the thrills and spills that come with family life. His wife, Tina, claimed to speak the worst English of all of them but was brilliant nevertheless. Their kids, Andreas (14), and Anja (12), were bright and funny and found nothing more victorious than correcting their parents' English.

For the last three years they had lived in Saudi Arabia; a country, according to their stories, unlike any culture I have experienced. For instance, Saudi law insists that women wear a long, black, loose cloak called an abayas that reveals none of the body below the neck including any suggestion of a woman's figure. The law also requires them to wear the head covering called a hijab and a face veil. "I never wear the hijab or... the thing over the face", Tina explained, "but I carry them with me in case I am stopped by the religious police".

"The what!?" I asked, somewhat alarmed.

"The religious police. They patrol the streets and make sure people are abiding by the religious laws." I had innocently considered religion to be a matter of personal choice.

The laws of women's attire are merely the cosmetic tip of a colossal inequality iceberg. Such is Saudi Arabia's contempt for women, if Tina were to be charged by the religious police, she wouldn't be charged... Karsten would! Tina wouldn't be to blame, or so it would be determined, the fault is Karsten's for he has not controlled his woman! *Desperately irresponsible, Karsten!*

There is a general principle in Saudi Arabia that forbids a woman to interact with an unknown man. Such carelessness is seen as a terrible crime and the height of misbehaviour. Their society invests a great deal of effort to prevent such an abominable event from occurring.

Also, Tina, by way of being born a woman, isn't allowed to drive and the law is supported by a number of well-considered arguments. For instance, if women were allowed to drive it might lead to them leaving the house more often. Or worse, the streets might become overcrowded and deprive young men from driving! Worst of all, so say the supporters of this law, they might be involved in a traffic accident, the worst outcome of which would be that she is forced into the presence of an unknown man.

And think of the precedence. If women were given the right to drive they might start wanting other rights. Where will it end… miniskirts?

Women are not yet allowed to vote (a restriction on women's rights that also exists in Vatican City, I might add). They cannot open a bank account, travel, seek employment or have surgery without the permissions of a male guardian. It made me wonder how frustrated Tina must get with the laws making her so dependent on her husband. Tina was even denied the company of her sister by a very particular Saudi Arabian immigration department. Usually not keen on letting anyone in the country, 'close relatives' are allowed to visit family but Tina's sister was not deemed close enough… to Karsten.

Tina and Anja seemed to be making a good fist of it and respected the customs of their host country. Perhaps never have I met more tolerant people, particularly when I learned that Saudi Arabia is, supposedly, a dry state - no booze for anyone. That is apart from the rich, powerful and influential who are able to circumvent the laws as it suits them. *Often the way, I fear.* Karsten got through it by brewing his own wine. There's no way he could get through it all without a little drink.

Saudi Arabia, however, is easing up a bit. Women look like they'll get the vote for their 2015 elections and be able to run for public office. Pressure is building for them to be allowed to drive (they already drive in rural areas through necessity and ignoring the law). It is possible to buy designer abayases with different cuts and colours and Tina quite enjoys shopping for them. Local girls wear western jeans underneath their abayas, apparently, and Tina says the religious police have never told her to wear her head covering or face veil, possibly because that would cause her to interact with an unknown man. It may also be because she is Western and allowed a little leeway. I have heard that any crimes committed against westerners are likely to result in a quick execution.

I suspect things will continue to change as the TV and internet allow people to learn how other people live and perhaps like different ideas.

With a commandeered decrepit bicycle from the guesthouse I flew down the main road towards Rawana falls. The road bent sometimes left and sometimes right, but always down.

It reminded me of a trip I enjoyed in the Peruvian Andes. A van drove us to the cold and misty mountain top where we were given bikes to cruise effortlessly down the mountain road with for a full two hours. (My Welsh singing friend, Arfon, had declined to come due to his vertigo.)

I coasted, looking for some good old-fashioned mischief. I cruised down the smooth road that clung to the mountainside, past a few small groups of mischievous-looking monkeys, until I reached the twenty five metre high flourish of gushing water that I had seen from Little Adam's Peak.

Dozens of locals had come for a look, a swim and a wash in the plunge pool. Courteous people were helping nervous people across the rocks and saying 'hi' to me. Some clever and arduous people had engineered showers by carving a plumbing system into the rock and a consistent flow of river water poured through three convenient showerheads. The system was even equipped with a stone water tank and carved overflow 'pipe'.

Well rested, I began my ascent back up the hill, aided by my decrepit bicycle hardly at all. The long and tortuous road bent sometimes left and sometimes right, but always up. The monkeys, passers-by and I all wondered what on Earth I was doing - Ella is a place for relaxation, not gruelling exercise. The further I went, the more exhausted I looked and passing locals began to applaud my efforts.

My burning legs and heavy breath caused me to rest for a minute or two and contemplate my foolishness before re-embarking on this arduous and pointless mission. I was overtaken by open-back vans full of local people hurling encouragement at me as they accelerated away. The cheers spurred me on and gave me the energy to reach Ella in a shattered, but victorious state. There was no doubt – *tonight I will treat myself to a chicken khottu.*

And a fine chicken Khottu it was too, for two reasons. Firstly, the chef in the open kitchen by now recognised me as a fervent customer and said "Ah, hello. Chicken khottu, yes?"

"Yes please", I confirmed, smiling and nodding.
"OK" he exclaimed, with the gusto of a man who knows he's about to impress. "How spicy do you want?" he asked, as any connoisseur would.
"Very very mild please. I can't take it too hot."
"I put no chilli in it for you, ha ha, how is that?" he suggested, laughing.
"Maybe just a very small amount", I offered.
"Ha ha. OK, just a little." Finally, a meal I could eat without my mouth being assaulted.

The second reason for this fine Khottu being so memorable is that it was accompanied by a mighty rainstorm that swept through Ella. It was already dark and the storm provided no thunder and lightning. Instead, it sent a heavy downpour of rain such as I had never seen. Within minutes the streets were rivers. The loud roar of rain lashing at the windows made it difficult to hear anything else and any wild-hearted souls who stepped outside were wet through in an instant. The power often cut out for a few moments plunging the small jungle town into eerie darkness. *This*, I thought, *is exactly the sort of dramatic weather we don't see in England.* Safe and warm, with my Chicken Khottu, I loved every bit of it. When the rain eased off I made the short dash back to my guesthouse.

Whilst playing games with my new Danish friends I was stunned into shock and despair as Anja described, in detail, how her friend's 13th birthday party had descended into chaos and violence following a deep and fundamental disagreement as to which was the superior, Justin Bieber or One Direction.

Both have their talents, I'm sure. Justin Bieber appears to have taken the pop world by storm without ever disturbing anyone over the age of 18 until it was too late. I first heard of him in the company of my Welsh singing friend, Arfon, who received a call from his 13 year old daughter asking for £30 to go to a Justin Bieber concert. "I'll pay for you to see The Who or The Rolling Stones" I overheard him plead before he reluctantly gave in.

One Direction is a boy band of four or five decent enough chaps, I suppose, forged together in the grasp of Simon Cowell and his X-Factor. These young gents managed the remarkable achievement in 2012 of winning a Brit Award for the Best British Single of the year with what was almost certainly the worst British single of the year.

From Anja's descriptions the hair pulling and scratching failed to resolve the issue but, more importantly, why weren't they arguing about two *proper* bands!? Sadly, they are not alone. Anja explained that there are well-populated social media groups having the same fierce argument the whole world over. The condition of kids' musical tastes is a disaster! *What the hell is going on?*

Although not quite as serious as all that, Anja's musical attention stretched little further than these two pop acts and would camp in One Direction's corner if push came to shove. "Karsten" I called, aghast, "you have to do something about this", but Karsten had the look of a man who has tried, tried and tried again and given up. The will of an almost-teenager is one to reckon with.

After breakfast, early the following day, I gave my farewells to the Australian and Dutch couples as they climbed into a taxi destined for blue whales. My day was to accomplish the strenuous climb of Ella Rock.

The Danish family had been to Ella Rock the previous day and young Andreas gave me a complicated set of directions. He was not the only person to tell me that the route up Ella Rock was a maze of paths, forks and turns with, oddly, no signs at all. It is possible to hire a guide, and therein lays the truth of it.

The cunning folk of Ella Rock keep their eyes peeled for tourists who may or may not be lost. The poor little tourist, uncertain and anxious at the prospect of being lost, has their fears confirmed when a friendly, all-knowing local fella pops up and tells them, indiscriminately, that they're going the wrong way whether they are or they're not. *Oh no! How on Earth am I going to find this place*, worries our tourist but fear not, for our local friend offers to guide them... for a small fee, the devious little rascals. This, my friends, is why there are no signs on Ella Rock.

Personally, I had no intention of ruining a perfectly good adventure by not getting lost. *An adventure without getting lost is no adventure at all,* I say. I resolved to make my own way, wrong turns and all. If all went well I'd find myself in all sorts of places I shouldn't be. And I reckoned I could get lost perfectly well on my own. I've been doing it all my life.

I will not acquire a guide, come what may, I vowed. With the super-efficiency of the three-toed sloth a guide would take me straight to the top of Ella Rock without any of the pointless detours or wrong turns. I'd miss the buzz of living off my own wits in unknown territory and the exciting risk of being stranded up the mountain all night... on my own. It would be like buying the answer to a crossword before you've even read the questions. *No no, I will be hiring no guides.* I'd only hire a guide if he could guarantee to get us both completely lost and in all the best places, but such guides are rarities.

I walked down the train track singing "stand by me" and looking for a left turn leading to a bridge. This bridge marked the full extent of what I had remembered of Andreas' directions. "Stand by me" was interrupted when a local farmer caught up with me to say, "Hello, which country?" I divulged *which country* and that my destination was Ella Rock and, in return, he divulged his secret of growing tomatoes. "Lots of sun and lots of water." *Hmmm, simple as that, eh?*
"It can be very difficult to find the way if you don't know it", he told me. "You could get lost." *Indeed.* He led me into his friend's bean growing farm where I studied the irrigation system, found a delightful hidden waterfall, a less delightful, unhidden lizard and a bridge as foretold by Andreas. At the far side of the bridge I faced my first navigational decision, left or right.

Just a minute later I was approached by a local guide. "You have gone the wrong way. You will get lost", he told me.
"Right you are", I said, changing directions.
"Hey, mister. I can guide you for a thousand rupees".
"No, no. I'm fine, thanks friend", I replied striding forth and left him with the wide eyes and gaping mouth of disbelief at what he had just witnessed.

Having no idea where I was my attention naturally turned to the job at hand. I meandered through a variety of terrains. Tea plantations evolved into narrow, stony, muddy paths through tall grass, light jungle and into open woodland that wouldn't seem out of place in England. The day was growing hotter, the climb steeper and the chances that I was going the right way diminished with every decision.

"Keep the top of the mountain in sight and head roughly that way", was Karsten's advice to me and it held me in good stead; that and choosing the steepest route at every decision.

Like Stephen Hawking's particles there were numerous different paths I could take; I just didn't find the shortest. I did, however, find a chameleon, a large bird of prey hovering overhead and a variety of butterflies and exotic birds fluttering and tweeting through the brush.

The steep peaty path was surrounded by tall and straight trees and increasingly interrupted by protruding boulders the further I climbed.

The last twenty minutes or so was a gruelling ordeal but my spirits were boosted by my faith that I was on the right track.

With the sense of triumph one gets from completing a maze I found the top of Ella Rock. It was marked by a vertical wooden pole where past conquerors have carved their names. I added mine into the timber. It is a beautiful spot for the well-earned gulps of water and biscuits.

The view opens out across the mountains of the hill country and the plains beyond. All is laid out before the weary conqueror just when he or she is wondering whether it was worth it and impresses that it was. I could see Little Adam's Peak across the valley and the little stone slab I had rested on the previous morning.

Finding my own way round the labyrinth to the top of Ella Rock was entertaining indeed and so was the descent. Five minutes down I bumped into Andrea – a doctor from Bristol, England about thirty, who was glad of the rest. She was a sturdy girl, somewhat astonishingly, as I learned she'd had a tragic and awful back injury two years previous rendering her unable to do anything physical. Now she was climbing Ella Rock.

She had no intention of stopping there either. In the days to come she was planning to go to Nuwara Eliya (Little England) and then make the late-night climb to Adam's Peak. I explained my plans to go to World's End, sadly missing Nuwara Eliya, before also climbing Adam's Peak – quite possibly on the same night as Andrea. I forgave her craven decision to hire a guide though he was favourable to the guide hired by a well-prepared group I encountered five minutes later.

"Hey man, it's hot isn't it?" said a Canadian fella with heavy-duty hiking boots, hiking trousers, sports sunglasses, an impressive camera and a ruck sack that indicated he was intending to camp up here for the week.
"Just a little. Don't worry, you're nearly there. I've just come from the top. It's straight up here – ten minutes max", I clarified pointing the way.
"Are you sure, buddy!?" said the Canadian, strangely doubting a man who had just been there. "Our guide says it's another half an hour over that way", and I turned to see his guide heading down a different path beckoning them to follow him before I filled their heads with meaningful information about the route to the top.

I left them discussing their plan of action and somehow retraced my steps to a place I'd never been before. *Bloody Hell!! I'd not thought to get lost on the way down!* What a bonus it was to get lost again and see a different part of the mountain. Perhaps it was the way I was supposed to go in the first place. I continued on and eventually found a train track, guessed at a right turn and soon found the small bean farm and bridge I went past on the way up.

My Danish friends were at the guesthouse on my return and invited me to join them for a farewell pizza dinner with them. I don't have a wife or children but getting to know a family like them was wonderful. They seemed very happy and I'm sure Karsten and Tina consider themselves very fortunate – most of the time.

I said my fond goodbyes and left to catch my train to Ohiya – the starting place for the trek to World's End.

Lord, I hope Anja starts listening to some decent music…

Chapter 18 – Train in the Hill Country

"A ticket to Ohiya, please?" I requested at Ella train station. I had arranged a guesthouse in Ohiya and a driver to pick me up from the train station, my cheap, rubbish phone coming in handy again.

"You can't buy a ticket now", was the reply from a tall plump station master.

"Pardon?" During a confusing conversation he managed to convey that he won't sell any tickets until thirty minutes before the train gets here, due at 19:05. It was a linguistic bridge too far to extract out of him the logic for that. At 19:20 he announced to the station that he was now happy to sell tickets and, an hour late, the train finally arrived.

On the train I was joined by three other travellers. In their mid 20s Heiko and Slawo were both active, strong looking Germans and were making the most of a break in their electrician course to travel around Sri Lanka. They were getting the train to Nuwara Eliya (Little England), another hour or two further down the track from Ohiya. I felt a little jealous. Short of time I had chosen to sacrifice Nuwara Eliya to fit in World's End and Adam's Peak.

The third fella, also mid 20s, was a Frenchman on his way even further down the track to Hatton. Nearing the end of his trip he was determined to squeeze in as much as he could by not sleeping. *A novel idea.* His plan was to get to Hatton, maybe about 2am, get a tuk tuk to Adam's Peak, dump his backpack in either a guesthouse or a bush and climb the thing straight off. "What - tonight!?" I remarked.

"Yez, of course. I don't have zee time to hang around", he explained.

The spectacular view of the jungle outside was wasted in the darkness, as was the view of the stations. There was no warning or announcement of approaching stations; instead they left us with the exciting puzzle to work out where to get off ourselves. The better-maintained stations branded signs at the front of the platform and, if particularly fastidious, on the platform itself.

I hung out of the open door to keep an eye out for Ohiya. "Ah, there it is!" The sign was nicely lit up to make things easy. As the train slowed I donned my backpack and strapped the rucksack to my front, wished the Germans a fun time in Nuwara Eliya and luck to the crazy Frenchman. When the train stopped I climbed down the steel ladder onto the track.

Where's the platform!? I thought. *I must have got out on the wrong side, although I saw the sign on this side. Where is it?* I couldn't see behind the train but there didn't appear to be a station here at all... *but I had seen it! Is this Ohiya? It just looks like I'm stood by the side of a train in the middle of the jungle at 10:30pm and the train will move off imminently.* I quickly trudged down the track towards the front of the train, laden with my bags, and shouted up to the driver, "IS THIS OHIYA?"
"?????????" he shouted back to me. *Blast!*
"IS THIS OHIYA?" I shouted up to him again. *What a stupid question. Of course it isn't, there's nothing here. I'm in the middle of nowhere.*
"?????????" he shouted to me again, or maybe it was something different.
"SHOULD I GET BACK ON THE TRAIN?" I asked.
"YES, GET ON, GET ON." *Ah, I heard that!* I walked back down the track to the first carriage and the first steel ladder. In the same second that I reached up to the first rung the train started moving and my flip flop fell off. *Christ, man!!*

I focused on what I was doing now - I didn't much fancy spending the night in the jungle. I unhurriedly put my flip flop back on to make sure I did it first time. *This is an emergency – don't get flustered*, I told myself. I ran a few steps to catch up with the ladder again. It felt secure in my hand so I leapt onto the lowest rung, careful to consider the weight of my backpack and rucksack strapped to my torso. The train was picking up speed, now 15mph. I felt comfortable enough, both feet on the bottom rung and firm grips on the ladder. I started to climb, one careful step at a time. I knew that if I fell it would be bad – certainly I'd be left in the jungle but to consider just how bad would be a waste of precious time. 3 steps, 4 steps, 5 steps... 25 mph, 30 mph. I escaped my concentration for a second to enjoy the thrill of the speed and the air rushing through my hair and over my skin as the train chugged round a bend.

I reached the door, let go with one hand to pull down the handle and pushed the door. It didn't move. I pulled the door outwards. It still didn't move. 35mph. My thoughts went back to the train to Ella, hanging out of the door taking in the views. It didn't scare me; I had done it before but maybe not quite like this and not carrying my bags. When no one was hanging out of the door it would bang away until someone locked the bolt. *Shit, it's locked with the bolt!*

Not wanting to disrupt people too much I politely knocked on the window of the door. I could just about see a fella lying down on the first seat sleeping soundly. He stirred slightly. I knocked louder. 40mph. He opened his eyes and saw me. *Thank God.* He rubbed his eyes, ambled over to the door and casually unlocked the bolt. I loved him for it. The door flung inwards and I stepped inside. "Thank you, friend" I said, smiling, and closed the door.

Sheepishly, I walked through the carriage to find the Germans and the crazy Frenchman. "Why are you still here?" asked Heiko. "Didn't you get off?"

"I did get off, but then I got back on again." I explained the shenanigans and came to realise that, one way or another, I had missed Ohiya and I was lucky to be alive, especially when Heiko mentioned the regularity of tunnels.

What now? It was 10:35pm and my guesthouse was to our rear. *I could get off at the next stop and get the train back. No way, there are only 3 trains a day. Maybe I could get off at the next stop and get a tuk tuk back? No, it's too far and too late. The next stop looks to be Nanu Oya, the station for Nuwara Eliya.* That presented Heiko and Slawo with their problem. To get to Nuwara Eliya one must get off the train at Nanu Oya and find a 30 minute tuk tuk ride. They had booked a guesthouse but were worried there wouldn't be any transport at midnight, the time they would now get there.

Right! Stuff World's End, it's gone. I'll call Heiko and Slawo's guesthouse and ask how to get from the station to Nuwara Eliya and ask if they have room for one more person. The kind sounding fella on the phone said that, even at midnight, there will be tuk tuks waiting at the station and he had a room for me. *Great!* And so I went to Nuwara Eliya with Heiko and Slawo instead. And what's more, they were as keen as mustard to grab a beer when we got there. My antique phone had saved me once again. Inevitably, Dammika was right.

Heiko was much the more talkative of the two Germans despite claiming that Slawo spoke the better English. He apologised for his English from time to time. I always feel ignorant and slightly ashamed when everyone else in the group speaks English because it's the only language I can speak. Whilst in Peru I went on a walking trip with a German guy, his Russian wife, a French couple, two Americans who spoke fluent Spanish and an Israeli girl. I thanked them all for speaking English all through dinner to which the German guy laughed and said they'd all be speaking English even if I wasn't there. English is the world's language of trade so people from different countries use English to speak to each other. If I was any other nationality than German Heiko and Slawo would be talking to me in English anyway. We English need not feel as ashamed as we often do in this respect.

At Nanu Oya, past midnight, the cold wind was complemented with spots of rain. We discovered a solitary tuk tuk with a tiny driver asleep inside. He had unrolled the plastic sheets and zipped himself inside to shelter himself from the rain. He awoke at our calling and pretended to be full of life as he helped us find a way to arrange three large men, three large backpacks and three small rucksacks into his tuk tuk before slumping at the wheel half asleep.

The journey through the darkness carried us down into the valley and up the other side towards Nuwara Eliya. We pulled over twice. "What's he doing?" we asked each other. It transpired he was refuelling from plastic bottles of petrol he casually kept under his seat. "Ok, ready to go now", he said trying to appear energetic, before falling half asleep again when he thought we couldn't see. Another exciting go in a tuk tuk; you always get more than you bargained for.

Heiko, Slawo and I shared a room in the spacious, pleasant guesthouse and the owner swiftly brought us a large beer each. Bier or beer – it was all the same beautiful stuff, especially after my eventful journey and it sank steadily until 1:30am.

Nuwara Eliya is known as Little England thanks to its English-summer feel of climate. It is cool and wet enough to grow strawberries, which is exactly what the British did to help them enjoy their occupation of Sri Lanka. Nuwara Eliya is where they fled when they could to escape the heat of the coastal areas. As a result the town prospered into the green and friendly place Sri Lankans go to holiday.

With time enough just for one day in Nuwara Eliya (population 26,000) it was a good, if unusual, thing for me to jump out of bed at 7am. Heiko was not a man for sitting around either; he liked to *do* stuff and suggested that we three active gents should set out to *achieve* something. Discerning visitors to Nuwara Eliya ordinarily enjoy a well-maintained golf course or perhaps a flutter at the horse track but the attraction on our radar was Sri Lanka's highest mountain – Piduruwatalagala.

The Lonely Planet book writes "Piduruwatalagala (2524m) rises behind the town. On top stands the island's main TV transmitter; the peak is out of bounds to the public." Our guesthouse owner confirms that we wouldn't be able to reach the very top but there are paths that lead to a waterfall. So, after breakfast we embarked on our quest to almost conquer Piduruwatalagala.

You may have just found yourself trying to say 'Piduruwatalagala'. It is a struggle for an Englishman, I'll admit, and requires some concentration. We knew it was inevitable that we would end up asking someone for directions and it fell to me to learn how to say it, a most satisfying accomplishment.

We moseyed into town down the wide and busy main street. The atmosphere was calm and agreeable; nothing was overly hectic or rushed, no one was in a hurry. Victoria Park, the town's primary green spot, sat on one side of the road with the golf course on the other. Further along was the central shopping area overloaded with liquor stores where we witnessed one fella down half a bottle of whisky and was promptly entered into my poll as loving his booze. This was April and the Sri Lankan holiday season had just begun.

Behind the town we saw the hills but couldn't discern which one represented our quest. We headed in the direction of the hills, into the back streets, left, then right, then left. "Excuse me, where is Piduruwatalagala?" I asked a few unknowledgeable people. Looking at the map we thought we knew where we were until we came to a dead end, a large, closed double gate restricting our progress. Behind the gate a large garden was being tended to by several gardeners and a narrow path ran from beside the gate skirting the edge of the grounds and up towards some grim looking housing.

"Hello! Hello…" we called. A half-naked man came to the fence by the gate. "Piduruwatalagala?" I said, and pointed down the narrow path to his right. The man looked confused. I tried again in my best Sri Lankan accent "Piduruwatalagala. This way?"

"No no", he said, looking slightly shocked, and pointed to his left far in the distance. "One moment", he said and disappeared.

"What's going on?" asked Heiko as we stood there, bemused.

"I don't know. He's gone but I think he'll be back. Maybe he's finding out how we can get to Piduruwatalagala." After a few minutes we heard the clang of metal behind the gate. It crept open and out came our friend and a skinny, dark man with a thin moustache, old smart trousers, flip

flops and a collared shirt under a hooded jacket. "This man will take you there", the first chap said.
"No no... no money" we said.
"He will help you, no money" the man said. "No money, no money" repeated the guide offered to us. *Oh, they're just being helpful.* "Ok. Thank you – lets go" and go we did.

The guide took off at a tremendous walking pace and, for some reason, it had to be so. Occasionally we three explorers unwittingly allowed our briskness to drop whilst in deep conversation or to look at something that caught our interest. Such behaviour was always met with a sharp "Come, come" from our guide. Even Heiko was disturbed by the swiftness we were prompted to achieve. "Come, come." *Ha ha, Bloody Hell,* "Yes, ok, ok". We walked the suburban streets with housing on either side and the hills began to climb to our left. Soon we started climbing too; the housing thinned and within ten minutes we reached a red and white striped barrier guarded by armed, uniformed men.

"Stop!" said one young man with dark, smooth skin and a slightly healthier build than our guide. We stopped. Where his comrades carried rifles he bore a handgun holstered at his waist and three stripes on his arm. "Piduruwatalagala?" I asked pointing up the mountain.
"You cannot go any more up", the young sergeant told us. We were nowhere near the top. I had expected that only the very top would be closed off, not damn-near the whole mountain. I wondered for a fleeting second if there might be some way round this blockade but quickly decided to agree with the men carrying guns.
"What about... is there a waterfall near here?" we asked.
"Waterfall? Er...yes, quite far." Our impatient guide intervened, obtained directions and began marching back the other way with renewed vigour to find us this waterfall. "Come, come!" We strode back down the road, skirting the mountain for perhaps a couple of miles before turning inwards onto a mountain path.

Surrounded by woodland and dense vegetation the path quickly grew narrow, rocky and steep. Brush sprawled across our way and it became apparent this trail was little used. We were taken down paths so overgrown we weren't sure they were paths at all, over rocks and boulders and through barbed wire fences. Slawo, Heiko and I began to suspect that our guide had never been here in his life. *He doesn't know where this waterfall is. He's winging it, this fella,* I kept thinking, but I enjoyed it nonetheless.

There is a deep excitement in being guided by a guide who doesn't know where he's going. We had somehow picked this stranger up that morning and bestowed upon him all decision-making responsibility. Sometimes we could see him pause, look around and ponder and I became more excited the more I thought he didn't have a clue where he was taking us.

He did, however, harbour a degree of talent. He found paths that weren't there, scaled boulders we just didn't consider, in his flip flops, and cajoled us follow. "Come, come". Onwards, upwards and downwards he took us through raw untouched undergrowth. This bizarre, scrawny, insistent little man found us our waterfall.

It was a sheer face of rock reaching up some sixty metres and a modest stream of water splashed down. At the bottom, beneath the spray, loomed the plunge pool with swirling, gushing water that looked treacherous to anything embroiled with it. To the side of the plunge pool, propped against the cliff face, was a huge boulder some thirty feet tall, sat on top of which was another, smaller boulder. We scrambled over a collection of rocks in front of the plunge pool to get good views of the waterfall and closer views of the plunge pool. We caught our breath, took our photos and drank our water.

What next? We had achieved what we set out to as best as the Sri Lankan army would allow. We glanced over to the thirty foot high boulder and saw our guide stood on top of it. *How did he get up there?* I pondered knowing full well that Heiko would come to the same conclusion as me - *if he could do it, so could we.*

It was far from easy. *This fella has done it in his bloody flip-flops!* On the outside edge of the boulder was a steep path of soil and rocks that had to be climbed more than hiked. Tree branches bordered the climb and aided our ascent. The top of the boulder, when we reached it, unexpectedly sloped backwards into the waterfall and the surface was made slippery by the spray. We shimmied across the front edge and waved to Slawo as he took photos of us. I looked down on Nuwara Eliya from the top of this boulder some forty feet above the plunge pool and considered, *this is an exciting adventure this guide has taken us on.*

Heiko and I eventually stood up to find our way down and saw the guide climbing a tree at the side of the highest boulder, and casually ambled on top of that one! "Where he goes, we go, Heiko. Them's the rules." The tree was another 30 feet tall and its trunk ten inches thick. I hauled myself up the tree until I could hook my feet on top of the higher boulder twelve feet higher and dragged myself up. Together we sat in the middle of the top boulder to show off our accomplishments to Slawo taking photos below. We had achieved everything we had wanted and more.

We made our descent through immense tea plantations and poor housing areas where roads were dirt tracks and houses were made of corrugated iron, wooden frames and plastic sheets. A popular technique was to secure the corrugated iron roofs into place by positioning large rocks on top of them.

Everyone we saw was welcoming, enthusiastic with their smiles, often showing off how many teeth they didn't have. One fella proudly showed us round his cow shed busily sheltering both of his cows. Groups of kids followed us, laughing and smiling; the brave ones said "hello" but they all loved having their picture taken.

Soon we reached the main road and began a thirty minute weary plod back to Nuwara Eliya's centre. Although we got nowhere near the top of Piduruwatalagala we felt thoroughly satisfied with our adventure so gave our diligent guide some money to thank him for his efforts.

Our few remaining hours in Nuwara Eliya were spent researching the best way to reach our respective destinations, having lunch in the park whilst a local fella sat at our table playing guitar and singing 'West Virginia', ' Let it Be' and others and poking around the markets where Heiko bought ten bananas for his journey to Kandy.

"Hatton, please" is all I said to a couple of people at the bus station and they pointed me the way to an air-con bus driver who let me sit in the front seat, much to the amusement of Heiko as I waved out of the window on departure.

I had enjoyed such a good day with Heiko and Slawo on my unexpected stop at Nuwara Eliya and we had managed to explore it well. It seemed amazing that, as my bus pulled away quite possibly never to see the two of them again, I had not even known them for 24 hours.

Chapter 19 – Adam's Peak

Hatton was, for at least the thirty minutes I was there, a dirty horrible depression, dark, smoggy and dusty. A tuk tuk driver found me at the bus station, I suspected having been tipped off by my hotel as to my arrival and need of a ride through the dark hills to Dalhousie - the small village at the foot of Adam's peak.

This wise old fella was a friendly, bubbly bloke with short-ish, scraggily, grey hair, a beard to match and an urge to talk and overcharge. "That's a bit expensive, friend", I said, "I'll go and ask that tuk tuk driver over there... or that one." *The laws of supply and demand hold sway.* As I walked off he beckoned me back with a more reasonable price. *I'm getting the hang of this... finally.*

The night-time journey through the wilderness was serene and mysterious as our tuk tuk motored along the dark, winding roads of the mountains. The experience was enhanced further by the view of Adam's Peak in the distance and the illuminated path that stretched crookedly up to its summit. According to this fella the journey required some rip-roaring, tub-thumping, dance or trance music vomiting out of his rear speakers. Against the back drop of the silent mountain range we were a tiny ball of energy blazing a trail through the dark tranquillity of the night. I soon encouraged him to switch the music off, a rewarding impulse as we later surprised a large mongoose scavenging in the road (the biggest the driver had ever seen) and an energetic wild boar. Apparently wild boars are common folk in these parts and sightings are regular.

Once at the hotel the driver chatted to the hotel manager whilst I was made welcome with a meal, a beer and a bed in preparation for a mountain climb at 2:30am.

I crept out of the hotel in the dead of night realising that only 25 hours ago I was unexpectedly arriving in Nuwara Eliya with Heiko and Slawo. Signs and bright lampposts guided the way to the foot of the climb along the wide dirt track lined with predominantly closed stalls. The rare open stall sold tea, coffee, water and biscuits. Anticipation rose slightly as, from time to time, I climbed a step. I knew the climb would soon be nothing but steps. *Step on every step*, I told myself. Smaller steps save strength, much like using a low gear on a bike.

Still half asleep, I heard voices ahead of me. No... it was just one voice. On and on that voice went from one tale to the next to the next.

Two people but one voice… it belonged to Edith and she used it at every opportunity. The recipient of Edith's voice was Mayaan, a girl Edith had met moments earlier and then I met the pair of them.

Both girls were very beautiful. Edith had straight blonde hair tied in a ponytail just past her shoulder, striking angular features and a fit slender physique. Mayaan was darker skinned with cute softer features, long and thick black hair and she too had a slender physique. *Adam's Peak, it seems, does have some power worthy of note.* We three, an Englishman, a German (Edith) and an Israeli (Mayann) advanced towards the temple at the top of the mountain.

Edith spoke a lot about travelling. She lived in Zurich, Switzerland and has been just about everywhere. Whenever a place was mentioned Edith had been there. For a girl in her late twenties she'd had a life that most 60 year olds would have been pleased with. She rows competitively, does triathlons and goes to great lengths to watch the German national football team in the World Cup. She was taking only a couple of weeks to travel around Sri Lanka and had hired a driver to take her round. Because the island is quite small and drivers quite cheap it's a popular travel option for tourists (not nearly as cheap as the bus, mind you). "I couldn't believe it", Edith said, "my driver followed me to my hotel room one night and asked if I'd like some extra services!"

Mayaan, like virtually everyone else on Earth, spoke less than Edith. She wore black professing that she used to think it made her look slimmer until one day she found it made her look just as fat as every other colour, seemingly ignoring the fact that she wasn't fat at all. (Every Israeli girl I have met, which is not many, is obsessed about their weight.)

Soon the climb became an eternal succession of steps. Cool air refreshed our faces as we pressed higher – Edith timing our climb to the top like this was some sort of sport. *These Germans seem obsessed with achievement.*

Sri Lankan people were also making their way up the stairs and, curiously, down. If the general idea is to get to the top in time to watch the sunrise, *what the hell is going on?* I can only imagine they wanted to reach the temple to engage in some prayer and didn't much care for the sunrise. Occasionally we passed a frail old-timer struggling to climb up or down the steps, whichever was their particular inclination. If this was their effort to complete a Sri Lankan person's ambition to climb Adam's Peak at least once in their lifetime it seemed like spectacularly poor planning to me. In the event they were generally accompanied by a contingent of dedicated sons and grandsons to half-carry them along.

The temple complex at the top covers about forty metres square and a tiny traditionally-decorated shrine housing a few Buddha statues is raised in the middle. Pilgrims step inside for just a few seconds to make their prayers. *A long journey for just a couple of sentences,* but that might be the point of it. Beyond the temple's boundary wall are great stretches of Sri Lankan hill-country in every direction.

Everyone who has been up Adam's Peak advises you to take warm clothing because it gets cold up there. In a country almost exclusively bathed in sweat-dripping heat one wonders how cold is "cold". The truth of it is it's bloody freezing! I wore a t-shirt, woolly jumper and hoody and was still shivering. Local families huddle together under sheets and blankets trying to retain some warmth whilst the occasional lone shiverer retreats deep under whatever shelter they brought. As is deemed respectful, we removed our shoes and socks to enter the temple grounds, Edith being rather pleased to show off her painted toe nails despite the chill. The cold tiled floor soon willed her socks back on, I noticed.

Most people, rather oddly, gathered towards the south wall to watch the sunrise, whilst I thought it was commonly understood that the sun rose in the East. As such we worked ourselves into a good East-facing position as the sky began to turn from black to dark blue.

Soon the first hints of red and burnt orange leaked onto the threads of cloud above the horizon. Then a crack of gleaming yellow and an array of oranges and reds whispered above the distant mountains and contrasted with a variety of deep blues in the clouds above. Two minutes later the cloud formations had altered offering another unique image – a spectacular sunrise, different every day and I'm told that it can be even better.

In the right conditions a shadow of this conical mountain is cast onto the clouds on the opposite side. The sun comes up so fast in Sri Lanka it is possible to watch the shadow lower as the sun rises. You are lucky if you manage to catch a view like that.

There are seven different paths up this mountain. It is easy to find the way up, you just follow the path to the top, but finding the right way back down is a trickier proposition when there are seven paths and the ascent was spent half asleep and in darkness. I know now that we chose the right path but there were bridges, rivers, boulders and forks that I had no memory of. I reckon it was a good job I had a German with me.

What I didn't realise was that my German was one of those lie-through-yer-teeth, bullshitting, "this is the best thing ever" Marketing people!! As delightful, beautiful and interesting as she was, when she told me she was in marketing it was all I could do to not throw her off the mountain. Instead I reluctantly trod a fine line of outwardly smiling whilst my insides boiled close to a violently explosive rant about marketing departments and their remit of impressing falsehoods onto the good public.

Edith's particular brand of marketing was rather interesting and terribly disturbing. She worked for Mont Blanc, a reputable maker of exquisite watches, wallets, pens, pen pouches (???), leather bags, jewellery and the like. However, Edith's speciality blows the mind far beyond this lot. Edith sells pens for twenty thousand pounds each!!

Mont Blanc would design a new, top of the range, stylish pen and give it name like 'The Einstein Pen' and then only make about 100 of them, *the laws of supply and demand hold sway.* Edith would then market these to, what I presume to be, absurdly rich people with an equally plentiful amount of stupidity. You might think that these stupid, rich people might enjoy writing with this magnificent pen, and I'm quite sure the pens write splendidly, but most don't use the pen at all.

These people are collectors. Mont Blanc, in a cunning marketing ploy, place a manufacture number on each pen and that appeals to the nature of collectors who become obsessed with having collections of items each with specific manufacturing numbers. In turn, Edith markets new products with certain manufacturing numbers to people she knows collect those numbers. "I have an exquisite pen with your favourite manufacture number, Sir", I suppose is how the conversion starts. The obscenely wealthy collectors then put their £20k pens in drawers, safes or cabinets and sleep soundly at night in the knowledge that their collection of numbered exquisite pens is coming along nicely. Needless to say, I was flabbergasted.

But surely these rich folk can't be that stupid if they are obscenely wealthy, right? Why do they engage in such folly? I wondered if the collector's abstract sense of achievement was the only value the pens retain or whether there was some other benefit I had missed? Perhaps it creates a talking point in their household – something to impress visitors. "My oh my, look at that. Why do you have a collection of pens in your glass cabinet?"

"Oh those", they might say with swelling pride. "This collection of pens is worth over £200,000."

"Really!? My oh my, why *the hell* do you have a collection of pens worth over £200,000 in your glass cabinet?" I can't imagine a satisfactory answer. "Because they all have the same manufacture number", doesn't quite do it for me.

Maybe it's an investment and they can sell these pens for three times the value in ten years' time, I thought, but that would require some other rich clown to pay even more for a pen. And would they do it also in the hope of selling it on in a further 10 years' time, and who to?

I wouldn't have thought whatever buzz they get from this pen would be as fulfilling as donating £20k to a homeless shelter, or a children's home or cancer research... or the local frog and newt conservation society – anything but a silly, material collectable.

Mont Blanc has engaged their well-oiled marketing machine in a technique worthy of despise of a rare intensity. They have created a need. If your business can't think of a product to satisfy a need, why not create a new need and satisfy that? There is no greater feather in a marketer's cap than to create a need. To convince someone that they need something that they don't need is the Holy Grail in the marketing world and it's a horrible activity. Most people struggle to afford for all the needs they do need without having to pay for needs they don't need.

It's the taxi drivers at Colombo airport saying I needed them because there is no bus. It's the bloke who started ironing his shirts causing everyone else to iron their shirts too. It's the glossy magazines with airbrushed models on the front cover telling girls they need to be unhealthily thin and have beautification surgery. It's the loan companies who claim to solve your debt problems by giving you a loan at 4,000% pa. It's every advertisement that tells you that if you don't have their product then you are so insignificant you might as well not bother with life at all. It's the Mormons and Jehovah's witnesses that tell you if you don't convert to their religion then an eternity burning in the Sri Lankan Department of Immigration is what awaits you after your death, sonny (although I have no proof that that isn't true).

And what a remarkable accomplishment it must be to convince someone they need a pen to the tune of twenty grand. One can only imagine what spectacularly gifted, skilled and despicable people they must be! Had those innocent people been left alone I doubt they would have independently thought, *hmmm, I need a rare, finely engineered pen to not use, preferably with my favourite manufacture number and I will hand over around £20k for it?* Mont Blanc dangled this nonsense in front of clearly obsessive people who then became unable to go to bed and sleep soundly because their collection of numbered exquisite pens was *not* coming along nicely. I dare say they would have gone about their lives perfectly contently without expensive unused pens sat on their shelf at home – even if they did all have the same manufacture number.

Everything about Edith was delightful, fun and impressive in no small quantities. She performs her despicable job admirably allowing her to enjoy adventurous holidays, explore the planet and flourish in one of the most expensive cities in the world. She is encouraged to wear Mont Blanc merchandise both in and out of work so that she can talk about it should anyone show a bit of interest. Not me though – she hadn't worn any at Adam's Peak and I hadn't the taste for it.

As it turned out Edith would shortly be driving to Colombo to stay in the very swish Mount Lavinia Hotel – the large white hotel just down the beach from Dammika's. We would both be there in a couple of days so we arranged to meet up on Wednesday evening for a meal.

At the bottom of the mountain we said our farewells, swapped phone numbers and went our separate ways. *Now off to bed!*

I awoke and ate a late lunch in the hotel restaurant where I discovered Doctor Andrea (from the top of Ella Rock) and some amiable gentleman she picked up at World's End. Whilst my plans to go to World's End changed during the exciting train station mix up, Andrea had somehow changed her plans and ended up at World's End. I arranged to meet Andrea and her new chum in the restaurant for dinner at 6pm and went off to investigate the little town I was staying in.

We were approaching the Buddhist New Year and some excited revellers could hold their patience no longer. The whisky bottles were open and dancing ensued to the terrible music of the DJ and band that defiled the stage.

I remained at the furthest end of a flat dry field to the stage and discovered a curious game that some of the male festival-goers were embroiled in. A tall, wooden telegraph pole stood thirty feet out of the ground and, fully equipped with an old rag, each participant would climb this pole using the magic of friction and mark the pole with chalk as high as they could. Getting down unharmed was as much of a skill as getting up. *Such inventiveness.*

At 6pm I was half way down a beer waiting happily at a table for Andrea and her new friend, Martin, whilst watching a storm roll in and roll out again. They eventually arrived with apologies for oversleeping but it mattered not as I had all the time in the world and another beer.

Andrea was the sort of girl who was always very nice and courteous, cleanly spoken, careful and unwaveringly polite. Martin was even worse. As we chatted about our travels I drank beer, they drank water, eager to avoid a heavy head for their night-time climb.

They didn't offend me in any way. They didn't even come close. Nor did they say anything offensive about anyone who wasn't there. I don't think the pair of them had insulted anyone in years, not even accidentally such was the cautious nature of their dispositions. I wondered if they had ever done anything awkward to explain in their lives. *A life without silliness is not a life worth living.*

Neither in the mood for beer or silly conversation they retired to bed early despite my witty repartee and left me alone with my fourth pint. A cynical man might suggest they had a dirty little secret that was best kept behind closed doors... bedroom doors. A cynical man might suggest that Martin displayed the sickeningly sweet chivalry only found in men with more wicked deeds in mind.

Fortunately for me there were four young women at the next table who were keen on both beer and silly conversation so my cynicisms and I spent the rest of the evening with Jen, Amanda, a Canadian, and a maths teacher. They were preparing for their night-time hike using the alternative technique of heavy boozing. *This is more like it.* I drank the evening away with these four potty-mouthed, gossiping, impulsive and slightly saucy hedonists, never to see them again.

Chapter 20 – Colombo (Part 3)

With the help of four blustering buses I arrived close to Dammika's house some eight hours after my 8am start and with a strong desire for a shower. The journey was passed, in part, chatting with a seventeen year old Sri Lankan lad on his way to Colombo to spend the Buddhist New Year with his older sister. A very pleasant young lad, he was polite, interesting and curious. He asked me if I had a girlfriend. It turned out he didn't have one either.

Things rarely go how they are expected to when travelling. In fact, expectation is a hobby of folly. Laden with my bags I trudged down Galle Road looking for a shop that might sell me some shower gel when a group of playful young Sri Lankan lads casually walked towards me. I had grown accustomed to groups of young lads looking at me, whispering to each other and breaking into fits of laughter. I couldn't blame them for it either. I'm quite sure I was often looking, or doing something out of place that gave rise to some point of humour I knew nothing about.

In this instance one smiled and said to me, "Hey man, tsunami... here... now", and they all laughed. *Ah, playing on the ignorant western conceptions of Asia, eh? Tsunamis all the time, is that the way of it? Very funny mate.*

Five minutes later, having bought my shower gel, I walked out of the shop and into the presence of a local policeman. "Hey, you know, tsunami coming", he said tapping his watch, "in forty five minutes!!" Now then good reader, I don't know about you but my experience of the police playing practical jokes on the public was zero, in Sri Lanka or anywhere, so I decided to escalate the priority of this matter to a more urgent status.

Oh fuck! Don't panic, don't panic, screamed Jonesy from Dad's Army inside my head. It was perhaps the four weeks travelling through the unknown, the experience of the train to Nuwara Eliya or my confidence in Dammika's hospitality but I found to my own surprise that, for a life threatening situation, I remained quite calm. And anyway, I was looking forward to this shower.

As I walked through the back streets to Dammika's, people were scampering the other way carrying bags of food and telling me that a tsunami was coming. *What is Dammika doing?* I wanted to ask but expected they either wouldn't know Dammika or reply that they "wouldn't know what that crazy old goat would be doing."

I began to feel a little alarmed. Images of the mighty 2004 tsunami came to mind. 35,000 people in Sri Lanka died and a total of 230,000 people throughout Asia. It was of no surprise to see people stirred into action.

I reached Dammika's with 35 minutes left, according to the policeman's report - *I hope Dammika is home... I hope Dammika has a plan...!!*

"Ahh, Gavin!! Come, come!!" Dammika urged, very excitedly. "I have a cold bottle of beer for you!" *Great... I think.*

"Dammika, people are telling me that a tsunami is coming!" I exclaimed.

"Yes, yes, it's all over the news, come and see." Inevitably he was right. The news reported that, in fact, there would be two tsunamis. *Great!* An earthquake of 8.6 magnitude was soon followed by one of 8.3, both off the coast of Indonesia, only some 250 miles from the 2004 earthquake. Tsunami warnings were in place and people were heading to high ground and using inland roads instead of the main coastal routes. Bus and rail services on the coast had been suspended, including the train line Dammika had sent me to walk down on my first stay with him.

Dammika had set up his radio in the living room and talked to other radio users around Sri Lanka. "When satellites stop working, and internet stops working, radio will still work," I recalled Dammika telling me. His radio pals gave regular updates of no dramatic occurrences yet.

"Dammika, what are we going to do?" I asked.

"Ha ha", Dammika smiled, "Nothing, Gavin. There will be no tsunami." I turned back to the news.

"The first Tsunami is expected to hit Sri Lanka in 25 minutes and another one a short while after that", reported the smart news broadcaster. "Tsunami warnings have been raised around the coast of Sri Lanka, Indonesia, Malaysia..."

"Dammika, are you sure?" I asked. "The news is saying that..."

"Yes, I'm sure", he interrupted. "They don't know, but I know."

Well, there you have it then, nothing to worry about, but just in case I negotiated for us to watch the tsunami from Dammika's roof. *Wouldn't that be amazing?* With plans now in place I started on the bottle of beer and popped onto Dammika's computer to tell my family not to worry about the impending tsunami they may have seen on the news, I am on the coast but my guesthouse owner says the news reports are wrong and he has it all in hand. We are looking forward to watching the whole thing, when it comes, from the guesthouse roof. With still a full fifteen minutes until the tsunami was due I went to have my shower so that I could either witness the spectacular show, or die, feeling clean and comfortable.

With two minutes to go we changed our plan and sauntered down the deserted street to the beach that the police had declared off-limits. This was Dammika's territory; the sea had been his Lord for twenty years whilst working on the ships. He would know. The sun was low by now and the beach looked quite beautiful with the coloured sky reflected on the calm waters. It all looked perfectly safe to us.

Two hours after the tsunami didn't appear the news reported that the tsunami warning had been lifted. Inevitably, Dammika was right. How lucky it was for me to witness the first real-life use of Sri Lanka's Tsunami Warning System. Their emergency procedures worked tremendously well. Everybody knew that a Tsunami was coming well before it didn't. The beaches were closed, beachside restaurants were closed, power was cut and the coast-line train was suspended. All areas where the Tsunami didn't come were evacuated and most people fled to high ground. Dammika took a photo of me in the sea exactly when and where the tsunami wasn't.

The preparations Sri Lanka had made since the devastating 2004 tsunami were proven an overwhelming success; the results of the Tsunami Warning System were outstanding. Not one person died during the crisis and no one had been injured as a direct result of a Tsunami. Let's hope their results are at least as good the next time they don't have a tsunami.

The question remains, however, after two earthquakes of 8.6 and 8.3 magnitude, why wasn't there a tsunami or two???

I was to spend the evening with Edith. She was running late into Colombo because of the tsunami, her driver having taken her to high ground. Most restaurants had closed for the day so we arranged to meet at the very grand and impressive Mount Lavinia Hotel where she was staying.

What better way to start the evening than to walk to the hotel down the beach? Once at the beach, looking left the hotel was lit up like a beacon in the darkness. Despite the day's earlier furore the sea remained tranquil, unmoved, unconcerned. What was a gentle breeze now blew a little stronger and the warm air that blew over my skin still had a slight charge of excitement from the earlier drama.

On approach to the hotel it became apparent that the way was cut off by waves, rocks and a stone wall too high and smooth to climb. *Blast!* I looked for a way off the beach but to my surprise and frustration there was nothing obvious. The best I could find was a small, closed café at the back of the beach where, with no small effort, I climbed a stack of chairs, over a wooden fence, under barbed wire and onto the train track. The ordeal left me sweaty, filthy and late. I rushed along the train track looking for a way onto the streets and found only high fences on either side. I then discovered I wasn't the only person there.

"Hello, which Country?" A young, skinny fella with a cloud of curly black hair and a shifty manner came ambling up to me. "Which country?" he repeated.

"Erm, I'm trying to find a way to the Mount Lavinia Hotel", I said. He pointed up ahead and to the left where I saw, through the darkness, a column of steps beside a bridge. "You want some marijuana?" he said.

"No thanks", I returned.

"Opium?" It seems you can't even ruin a dinner date before you've got there without being offered drugs round here.

I trotted up to the high, white walls of the hotel and through the heavy wooden and glass doors feeling like a piece of trash dragged in by a stray dog. I was welcomed by the hotel attendant contrastingly dressed in a flawless bright, white suit. I felt sure that if I couldn't speak English he would have thrown me out the back door with the kitchen waste and a swift kick in the backside.

To my dread Edith was waiting in the lobby looking fabulous and pristine compared to my filthy and dishevelled. "Hi Edith, I've accidentally had a small adventure on the way. I'm sorry, I'll just pop to the washroom."

We decided to eat fish in the 'Beach Hut', essentially a spacious, wooden restaurant on the beach with open sides and a thatched roof. Inside, hundreds of tiny golden lights and a few hurricane lamps gave a welcoming, rustic feel. Next to the open kitchen was an enormous blackboard offering every kind of fish I hadn't heard of and underneath that, displayed on a bed of crushed ice, was an array of curious looking sea creatures. Some looked appetising whilst others looked nothing short of villainous and extremely angry – perhaps not surprising under the circumstances. You wouldn't see cartoon adaptations of these fish cast as the hero in a Disney movie. They fashioned long, sharp spines on their backs and spikey teeth half the length of their body that convincingly said "fuck off" to anyone who happened to approach.

We questioned the chef at length about the fish and the ordering procedure. In general it goes like this; first you must choose a fish, then choose how to have it cooked (fried, deep fried, sauteed, devilled, grilled, poached), then what sauces to have with it (barbeque, mayonnaise, lemon mayonnaise, sweet chilli, garlic) and finally to choose french fries, wedges or some other form of potato. My knowledge of what each fish was like and how it should be cooked was zero so if it was left to me our dinner would be in the hands of the fates.

Edith, thankfully, seemed to know exactly what to do including which sauce should accompany which fish, and took charge. We eventually chose to share two unknown fish, one deep fried and one grilled, and Edith chose some sauces.

The English and the Germans are both hailed for drinking beer and we had been looking forward to a drink, especially after the thrills of the tsunami alert. When our beers came the waiter began to pour but Edith took charge. "Stop please. I will pour them," she informed us. "They never pour it properly," she explained before the waiter had gone. It was refreshing to see a German girl take care of her beer like the French do their wine.

We talked about our various travels. Edith doesn't always travel in such luxurious style as the Mount Lavinia Hotel. She had meant to be here with her boyfriend but they had split up not long previous. Usually she backpacks around which explained why she didn't seem overly disgusted with my ramshackle appearance. She told me about hiking in Nepal where young boys and skinny men had calf muscles like watermelons from carrying bags up the mountain every day. They would take tourists' backpacks up and watch the unburdened tourists struggle. She told me about Borneo and the climbing, water sports and endless activities that can be done there.

Interestingly, Edith described how she sometimes gets a small pang of nervousness when she tells people she is German. People still think of the war and, upon meeting a stranger, no one ever knows what nationalistic views and prejudices people harbour. I remembered Heiko mentioning that he would like to see London but was afraid to visit because he thinks he might get attacked for being German. What a sorry reflection of London and England it would be if there was a serious risk of that. After all, Edith and Heiko didn't fight in any war, they weren't even alive and neither was I. In fact, people still alive who did fight or suffer in World War II are very few indeed. It's a shame Edith and Heiko feel that modern Germans still carry that burden. Times have changed. A country's history, after all, is inherited. "Dear next generation of Germans, we hereby hand the country over to you. Erm... sorry about the mess. We made a bit of a pig's breakfast of it our end. There were a couple of wrong 'uns amongst us. Hope you have better luck."

"I don't think this lemon mayonnaise goes well with this fish", said Edith. "It's the wrong flavour, shall we get another sauce?"
"Get whatever you like, Edith", I replied. Edith took charge and immediately raised her arm to attract the waiter's attention but he wasn't looking. Unperturbed she kept her hand held straight up and carried on talking to me as normal. Well, this was new to me. I would have felt like a right tit if it was me but Edith seemed completely comfortable, like it was the most normal thing in the world. *These German girls are formidable indeed.* I struggled to concentrate on what she was saying, looking at her talking to me with her arm stuck in the air – how peculiar. But why did I find it so odd? It was completely logical. We want to attract the waiter but don't want to stop our conversation, so we'll carry on talking with Edith's arm stuck in the air. It can only be that I'm just not used to it, I suppose.

"So, how is it your ex-boyfriend didn't come in the end?" was the best way I could think to see if she wanted to talk about her ex-boyfriend. It was virtually the last thing I said to her. She told me the whole story and it is a tale of woe and villainy. I didn't catch the ex-boyfriend's name so let's call the low-down dirty cheating rat, Roland.

They were close and living together until Edith found evidence that he had slept with yet another woman whilst away on a business trip. She asked him about it and he confessed... again. This time Edith had had enough. She had found out about dirty Roland's unfaithfulness two or three times before and each time Roland confessed, apologised profusely, skilfully talked her round with claims of 'just meaningless sex' and promises of faithful adoration. He admitted to being a 'sex-addict' and offered to have counselling for his *illness*. Ultimately it was to no avail and possibly never taken seriously.

Roland's shame and self-torment for hurting his own girlfriend with as wicked a blow as he could possibly wield was clearly not enough to stop him from wielding it again... and again. How many were there, I wonder, that went undetected? How many more times did he risk

Edith's pain for 'meaningless sex'? And feel the same pain she did, three or four times in all. She forgave him, continued to love him and gave him more chances than he deserved to keep her but he gambled away her faith, love and kindness and rewarded her with more hurt. What kind of man is so cruel to the girl he loves three times? It seems one can be as soulless and heartless as a stone but still have everything women are attracted to. I swear I'll never work it out.

She is well rid of Roland but she sorely misses the warm, glowing and radiant feelings that he once gave her. I hope she never goes back to him longing for those feelings again but instead finds them from another more genuine source.

Walking back to Dammika's (on the roads) I thought of Edith and her life. She had talked for over an hour about Roland the bastard. She works so hard to squeeze every ounce of enjoyment and success out of life from travelling the world, her rowing club, keeping lots of friends and doing thy bidding for the Marketing Devil. She even gave her relationship with Roland every possible chance. She is made of stern stuff is our Edith and I hope she will see better relationships before long.

It was another early morning at the bus stop near Dammika's and, thankfully, bereft of prostitutes. My bus charged along the empty streets of Colombo as intensely as ever. My air-con bus to the airport dawdled annoyingly trying to pick up passengers who frankly just didn't want to go to the airport no matter how much he pestered them.

I walked to the airport doors where they had placed, with ruthless efficiency, a security officer to check everyone's passport before letting them into the airport building at all. I handed him my passport, he opened it... in the middle... didn't turn to the photo page... afforded a glance at it... closed it and returned it. Somehow, this one man represented extraordinarily tight and extraordinarily lax security simultaneously. *Extraordinary!!* Their security didn't stop amazing me there. I complied with the usual, dull, airport x-ray machine and frisking procedures, boarded the plane and, in reaching into my hand luggage for my Ipod, found my penknife! Oops.

Before I leave Sri Lanka behind I can tell you that out of the sixteen Sri Lankans I asked if they liked booze, eight (exactly half) did. Out of the eighteen I asked if they liked cricket, all eighteen loved it. In

Sri Lanka, cricket holds sway. It is just peculiar that their official national sport is volleyball!

I had also found in abundance the two things I had come searching for. Firstly the blue whales, of course. Plentiful are they. It turns out that those people who predicted that they might have a chance at survival if we stop killing them all were right after all.

Secondly, I wanted to discover and delight in behaviour the local people considered perfectly normal but was entirely unusual to me and gain an understanding as to why on earth these things go on. It was the umbrellas in the sunshine, the red stuff being spat all over the country, the several dozen elephants marching down the street, Edith sticking her hand in the air through dinner, bribery, cricket being shown in the supermarket, the general disinterest in having possibly the best place on Earth to see blue whales on their doorstep, the acceptance of pedestrians on a train track, all manner of behaviour that happens on the country's roads and the unconcern of officials when people travel either partly or completely on the outside of a train.

It's the reason I travel. To witness someone doing the most extraordinarily bizarre things and have them logically explained and being convinced that it is, indeed, a worthwhile activity. To me these are the real jewels of life.

On flying out of Sri Lanka I hoped that the second half of my Asian adventure would deliver much more of it. I would meet, and have chance to solve, more cultural mysteries like why those two tsunamis didn't arrive, would be inspired to ponder matters one doesn't ordinarily consider and meet people of spectacular peculiarity.

I was quite unaware how much my journey through Thailand, Laos, Cambodia and Vietnam would change me. After seven weeks I would return to Sri Lanka a thoroughly experienced Asian traveller, wiser in the scams and pitfalls of modern Asia and how to deal with them, but more than that, I was to find and gradually adopt the outlook that helps make the most out of travelling. I finally saw Colombo properly and much more of it than I'd bargained for. Travelling through unchartered territory held no fear; I was a transformed traveller. Things just worked.

The sequel to this book, 'Curious Chronicles from Indochina', completes this journey through time, space and humanity. I would be delighted for you to join me on this adventure too.

THE END

P.S. Should you wish, you can browse through a few photographs of what you have been reading about at www.facebook.com/curiouschronicles.

Bibliography

'A brief history of time' – Stephen Hawking

'A briefer history of time' – Stephen Hawking

'Sri Lanka' – Lonely Planet

'Vietnam, Cambodia, Laos & Northern Thailand' – Lonely Planet

http://whc.unesco.org/en/list/202

http://en.wikipedia.org/wiki/Sigiriya

http://investorplace.com/2012/09/least-fuel-efficient-cars-to-own/11/

http://boingboing.net/2010/01/21/four-fun-facts-about.html

http://www.sloth.gr.jp/1.Life.htm

http://www.botanicgardens.gov.lk/peradeniya/

http://www.wildlifeextra.com/go/whales/blue-whales-underwater.html#cr

http://www.sundaytimes.lk/120805/plus/sri-lanka-best-chance-for-sperm-whale-super-pods-7800.html

http://www.metacafe.com/watch/9163614/top_5_80s_cult_sci_fi/?source=playlist&passiveNav=1 –

http://www.nytimes.com/2012/07/03/science/traffic-in-sri-lankas-waters-threatens-blue-whales.html?pagewanted=all&_r=0

http://natgeotv.com/za/blue-whale/feature-articles

http://www.abovetopsecret.com/forum/thread795102/pg1

http://www.telegraph.co.uk/travel/destinations/asia/srilanka/8453749/Spotting-blue-whales-in-Sri-Lanka.html

http://www.expertcore.org/viewtopic.php?f=13&t=3537

http://blogs.discovermagazine.com/badastronomy/2011/03/31/the-earths-lumpy-gravity/

http://en.wikipedia.org/wiki/Blue_whale

http://latimesblogs.latimes.com/unleashed/2010/02/blue-whales-are-singing-in-a-lower-key.html

http://www.enchantedlearning.com/subjects/whales/species/Spermwhale.shtml

http://en.wikipedia.org/wiki/Sperm_whale

http://www.wired.com/wiredscience/2010/02/sperm-whale-teams/

http://www.science20.com/squid_day/do_sperm_whales_use_sonar_stun_giant_squid

http://www.oceanicresearch.org/education/wonders/spermwhales.htm

http://news.bbc.co.uk/1/hi/8530116.stm

http://www.youtube.com/watch?v=DArqBmkO_p0

http://www.livescience.com/7297-whales-attack-squid-mystery-deepens.html

http://www.nytimes.com/2012/07/03/science/traffic-in-sri-lankas-waters-threatens-blue-whales.html?pagewanted=all&_r=0

http://www.tonywublog.com/20120518/dead-blue-whale-ship-strike-sri-lanka.html#axzz29e5743bF

http://www.thesundayleader.lk/2012/03/25/blue-whale-collides-head-on-with-speeding-ship/

http://blogs.independent.co.uk/2012/05/11/to-avoid-more-whale-deaths-ships-must-slow-down/

http://www.scientificamerican.com/article.cfm?id=how-do-whales-and-dolphin

http://en.wikipedia.org/wiki/Women's_rights_in_Saudi_Arabia

Printed in Great Britain
by Amazon